Learn Talmud

BY JACOB NEUSNER

BEHRMAN HOUSE, INC.

Library of Congress Cataloging in Publication Data
Neusner, Jacob, 1932–
    Learn Talmud.
    English and Hebrew.

    SUMMARY: A study of the Talmud that applies traditional values to modern life.
    1. Talmud—Study—Text-books. [1. Talmud. 2. Jewish religious education] I. Title.
BM504.7.N48   296.1'206   79-9415   ISBN 0-87441-292-7

For
Irving Mandelbaum

ACKNOWLEDGMENTS   My thanks go to those who shared in making this book: Linda Altshuler, copy-editor; David Altshuler, coordinating editor; B. Barry Levy, linguist; Ed Schneider and Katherine Jungjohann, designers. Prof. Levy took full charge of the Hebrew text.

J. N.

PREFACE

The Talmud is part of the whole Torah that God revealed to Moses, our rabbi, at Mount Sinai. The Talmud is different from the other part of the Torah, the Hebrew Bible, and it asks for a different kind of learning. But it, too, is Torah. It tells us about the world God made.

That part of the world about which we learn, specifically, concerns the order and right way for our lives and our minds. The Talmud teaches us how to analyze what we do and what we are. When we enter into its ways of thinking, we follow a path that leads us to the mind of God who made the world and gives Torah. For as we use our minds to reason and think about the world and what we do in it, we enter those ways of thought that begin *every day* at Sinai—in God's revelation of Torah to Moses. By learning Talmud, we continually receive the oral part of the Torah here and now.

You may know the book that precedes this one, *Learn Mishnah.* If you do, you will find that we review four passages of the Mishnah you have already studied. But we see them in a different setting. Then we proceed to learn how the Talmud analyzes these same passages. You therefore will see what you know from a fresh angle. And you will learn new things. If you do not know that book, you will still be able to follow everything in this one. This book is complete in itself.

I dedicate this book to my student and friend Irving Mandelbaum, because he lives his life in accord with the whole Torah of Moses, our rabbi. He is a teacher of Judaism through what he says and, more important, through what he does. I love him and take pride in his achievements.

J. N.

Contents

PART ONE

What is the Talmud?

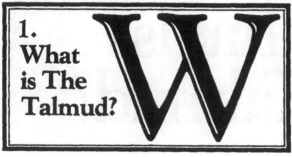

1. What is The Talmud?

What if someone asks you, "What is the Talmud?" Your answer may be short, or it may take a long time to find. The short answer is easy: The Talmud is an ancient Jewish book—actually a collection of many books—which came into being between the third and the seventh centuries of the Common Era, that is, about 200-600 C.E.

That answer tells us little. It does not tell us what is in the Talmud, what its components are, who made it up, or why. Most important: We do not know what to expect when we open a volume of the Talmud and look at it.

Why should I want to know what the Talmud is? Here a short answer is the right one: Because the Talmud is one of the two most important books in Judaism. The other is the Hebrew Scriptures, Tanakh.

Our religion is the religion of the Tanakh as completed by the Talmud. Tanakh without Talmud is not whole, but only a part of Judaism. The two together define Judaism. The reason is that God reveals Torah, and Tanakh and Talmud are the principal parts of Torah.

What about Mishnah? Where does it fit in?

In many ways the Talmud tries to answer that question. For the Talmud (that is, the Gemara; the two words mean the same thing) comes into being to make sense of the Mishnah. The Talmud wants to explain what the Mishnah means. When you open a page of the Talmud, the first thing you will notice is a paragraph of the Mishnah, followed by long, explanatory columns of the Mishnah and of laws, sayings, stories, and other kinds of discussion of the topic introduced, to begin with, in the Mishnah.

As I lead you through the Talmud, you will see that each passage of the Talmud we study begins with an explanation of the Mishnah-passage to which it is attached. Sometimes the Talmud will go on to expand and augment the Mishnah. At other times, the Talmud will take the theme or the subject of the Mishnah-passage and will tell us more things about that same subject. Often, the Talmud will then proceed to explain and expand what it already has told us about the Mishnah. So we shall watch for two processes:

explanation of the Mishnah, and *expansion* of the explanation of the Mishnah.

It is simple to picture how this happens. Imagine that you are giving a speech in Jerusalem, but you are speaking in English. Some people do not understand what you are saying, so someone stands up and proceeds to explain sentence by sentence and paragraph by paragraph the words you have used and then the meanings of your ideas and thoughts. The Talmud does essentially the same thing. It is a voice that follows Mishnah's voice, a second song. In some ways it sings the same tune—in some ways not—but it is always in harmony. It is like a conversation between a loud voice, Mishnah's, and a long answering call, the Talmud's.

WHAT THE TALMUD IS

The Talmud is a long explanation and expansion of the Mishnah. The Talmud is part of the "whole Torah of Moses, our rabbi," *because* it is attached to, and provides an essential explanation of, the Mishnah.

The Talmud is composed of two elements, therefore: a passage of Mishnah, followed by a long discussion of that Mishnah-passage. *Hence the Talmud is* (1) *the Mishnah and* (2) *the Talmudic commentary to, explanation of, the Mishnah.*

Notice, we have answered the question without turning to any matter of history. It does not really concern us when the Talmud came into being. We know that it was after the Mishnah was finished. What we want to know is why the Jews have thought, and now maintain, that the Talmud is worth their best thinking.

For after all, you do not need me to tell you that the Talmud is one of the key documents of Judaism. You have heard about the Talmud. Your rabbi has told you stories from the Talmud. You surely have listened to sayings from Pirqe Abot, the Sayings of the Fathers, a tractate of the Mishnah and thus part of the Talmud.

You probably also know that there are Jews, rabbis in particular, who spend most of their lives studying the Talmud in a yeshiva. They learn Mishnah and Gemara (Talmud). You may realize that many of the practices and beliefs of Judaism derive from the Talmud, or from the way in which the Talmud teaches us to read the Hebrew Bible.

7

So the Talmud, alongside the Hebrew Bible, is the most important book in Judaism. It is what makes Judaism special and distinctive. In the history of the Jewish people, from the time that the Talmud came into being, the Talmud defined Judaism both by the way in which it told the Jews to read the Hebrew Scriptures and by the way in which it told the Jews to live.

But merely hearing a book praised tells us nothing about it. What we really want to know is this: What do we find in the Talmud? What makes the Talmud special?

WHAT THE TALMUD DOES

In order to understand what the Talmud does, we have to remember what the Mishnah does *not* do.

The Mishnah rarely cites the Written Torah. It hardly ever quotes Moses.

The Mishnah instead quotes rabbis, people who are not mentioned in Tanakh and who do not speak in the name of God.

The Mishnah tells us the ideas of people who lived later than the time of the first Temple, before 586 B.C.E., or the time of the early centuries of the second Temple, after 500 B.C.E. The Mishnah speaks about people who lived in the first and, mainly, second centuries C.E.—a long time after the Tanakh was concluded.

Yet the Mishnah is called Torah—which is why the Talmud is Torah, too.

How can God reveal Torah at Sinai, so long ago, and yet speak through the rabbis of the first and second century whose words make up Mishnah?

That is one question which the Talmud must answer.

And it is the most important question in the history of Judaism—in the history of the Torah—from the creation of the Mishnah, toward the end of the second century, to the present day.

So one basic task of the Talmud is to find the source of Mishnah's ideas and laws in the written Torah, the Hebrew Scriptures.

SCRIPTURE, MISHNAH, AND TALMUD

Rabbi Judah the Patriarch sent the Mishnah out into the world without long quotations of Scripture. The Mishnah rarely quotes the written Torah, because Judah and his co-workers thought that the reason and the order in the Mishnah are enough. Truth is true, whether or not you turn to the written Torah to support your ideas. Reason is sufficient. Order is enough.

But as soon as people received the Mishnah and saw its immense and regular conception of the world, they realized that Mishnah was nothing less than a new Torah. It was, however, Torah produced by people whom they or their own parents actually knew personally. How can this be Torah, if Moses revealed the Torah long ago? Why should we take this thing seriously, if it is not revealed by God to Moses?

The answer to that question is not to toss out Mishnah because God did not give it. Nor is it to claim that God gave Mishnah to Judah the Patriarch. Judah and his co-workers were ordinary men. No one thought they were prophets or messiahs.

The answer of the great minds who received the Mishnah and began the Talmud is this: Let us show that Mishnah's truth is Scripture's truth. Let us demonstrate that Mishnah comes from Scripture. Nothing in Mishnah is different from Scripture. Nothing in Mishnah lacks a source in Scripture.

So the first generations of students of Mishnah, the great Babylonian rabbis (and some in the Land of Israel, too) who received the Mishnah and went to work to explain and apply it, had to do two things. (1) They had to discover the Scriptural basis for Mishnah's rules. And (2) they had to explain the meaning and message of Mishnah. The two kinds of work for those men really were one and the same.

What was the alternative? Why does the Talmud's discussion of so many passages of Mishnah begin, "What is the source of these statements?" And why is the necessary answer always, "As it is said . . . ," or "as it is written . . . ," that is, in *Scripture*?

Because of the alternative. For if the Mishnah is not Torah, then much that we believe to be Judaism—to be God's will for the Jewish people—is not revealed in Torah.

But if Mishnah is Torah, then God's revelation of Torah *continues* long after the moment when Moses went up to Mount Sinai to receive the Torah. In fact, what we mean when we say, "Moses received Torah at Sinai," is quite a different thing from what we might have imagined.

MISHNAH AND TALMUD

Mishnah claims to be Torah. The people who first learned and received Mishnah received it in the belief that it contained God's will. That is the fundamental, basic, and absolutely simple challenge before the rabbis—called *Amoraim* (*Amora* is the singular)—who created the Talmud. For their work was set out for them.

1. What does the Mishnah mean?
2. How is the Mishnah part of Torah?

Both questions are of equal importance. Torah is not gibberish. It is a set of important statements of what we should do and what we should strive to be. It is God's picture of us. Then should we not understand what those statements mean? Obviously, we must.

But at the same time, if Mishnah is part of Torah, then we have to be able to link Mishnah, the "oral" part of Torah, to Tanakh, the written part of Torah. So the Talmud comes into being to answer some formidable questions.

In telling you this much, I have told you too much. For what you really should do is find things out for yourself.

DON'T ASK—DISCOVER!

Why should information that comes to you easily mean anything? The best way to learn is to discover things on your own. That is why much about the Talmud is not spelled out in these past few paragraphs. Most of what you will want to learn is not said at all.

In this book you will work your way through each passage of the Talmud. But at the end, lest you forget the reason that you do this work, we shall ask ourselves: If *this* is Talmud, then *what* is Talmud? What is its purpose? What is its relationship to Mishnah? What is its message? Why is it important?

So from now on, you must not ask other people for answers, except to explain how a difficult word makes sense. You must find the answers for yourself. The great adventure of learning Talmud is the occasion and opportunity to discover things on your own.

That is why, for fifteen hundred years and more, the best Jewish minds have been devoted to study of the Talmud. To be a learned Jew means to know what is in the Talmud. To be a pious Jew means to keep what is taught by the Talmud. And whether you plan to spend many years studying the Talmud or have just this course to devote to that basic work of Judaism, the experience of learning Talmud must be the same: a chance to discover, to use your mind the way it is meant to be used.

HALAKHAH AND AGGADAH

In the pages that follow, as I told you before, you will learn four passages of the Talmud. These four passages illustrate different sorts of things you find in the Talmud, different kinds of things that the Talmud wants to tell us.

For the Talmud contains a great many more kinds of ideas than only interpretations of what the Mishnah says. It has, first of all, two completely different sorts of passages, (1) about what we are supposed to do, and (2) about what we are supposed to think and believe, about our emotions and our attitudes.

Passages about law tell us what we should do. They fall under the title, *halakhah*, from the word *halakh*, "go." The *halakhah* explains the way life should go on, the way we should do things.

Passages about beliefs, opinions, attitudes are called *aggadah*, narrative. *Aggadah* spells out the values and ideals that should guide us as we follow the way of the *halakhah*.

In this book, we shall have passages of a purely *halakhic* character, some of a purely *aggadic* sort, and some which mix together both kinds of material. In a given chapter of the Talmud, you are likely to find *halakhic* and *aggadic* discussion (in that order). It is unusual to find only *halakhah* or only *aggadah*. *Halakhah* is closer to Mishnah's contents—for Mishnah's literature is a nearly uniform set of laws, a statement of how things should be and are done. But *aggadah*—stories, wise sayings, statements of things you should believe and attitudes you should share and hold—is equally important.

In fact, one of the things you should look for, especially in Parts Two and Three, is the relationship between *halakhah* and *aggadah*. For the rabbis of the Mishnah and Talmud tell us to do certain things for a reason. And the reason has to do with things we believe. There is, therefore, a relationship between our actions and our attitudes, between what we are supposed to do and how we are supposed to see the world and understand our lives. We are what we do. But we do because of what we believe we should do.

If you see *halakhah* and *aggadah* as essentially separate, you will make a great error. You will want to know only one part of the Talmud, and not the other. There are Talmud-students who are interested only in the *halakhic* parts. There are others who want to learn only the *aggadic* sections. True, the former are sharper and more compelling. Equally true, the latter are easier to understand. They speak to us more directly.

But your work is not so easy. You have to understand the *halakhic* passage and the *aggadic* passage. And then you must ask yourself how the one and the other are related.

But that is enough talk *about* the Talmud. Now it is time to learn some Talmud.

2.
Don't Ask—
Discover!

This book will help you to meet the Talmud in its own setting.

That is, you will read the words of the Talmud, put together the way the Talmud puts them together. The alternative would be to cite some wise saying or some engaging story. There are many anthologies of sayings and stories. They tell us part of what is *in* the Talmud. They do not tell us what the Talmud *is*.

For the Talmud is not merely an anthology of this and that. It is a set of carefully worked out discussions, with a plan and a goal.

The Talmud does not merely string together wise sayings. It constructs arguments.

It does not merely tell stories. It makes points.

It does not provide interesting information alone. It conducts serious analysis of ideas and problems.

Now the Talmud is an extremely varied document. I have selected four sizable passages: Mishnah, then Talmud. The Mishnah-passages will be familiar to those who have studied *Learn Mishnah*. But they have to be learned once more. There are new angles here. And, of course, those who have now studied *Learn Mishnah* already know that, to study Talmud, you have to start with Mishnah. Then, following each Mishnah-passage, I present a large passage of the Talmud which is attached to that Mishnah-passage.

These sections of the Talmud that serve four Mishnah-passages do not give examples of everything you will find in the Talmud. But they give examples of important and common kinds of Talmudic discussion.

The first passage (Part Two of this book) is wholly legal, that is, *halakhic*. It gives us an idea of how the law of the Mishnah is analyzed by the rabbis, that is Talmudic lawyers.

The next passage (Part Three) is interesting for two reasons. First of all, it contains discussion of both law (*halakhah*) and theology (*aggadah*). Second, it is complete, not merely an excerpt like Part Two. Everything in the Babylonian Talmud about the Mishnah-passage will be before your eyes.

13

That will allow you to see how a complete discussion unfolds—beginning, middle, and end.

The third passage (Part Four) likewise contains both *halakhic* and *aggadic* materials. It explains the religious life of Judaism as we practice it today and is the most relevant to our own lives as Jews.

The final passage (Part Five) is mainly of an *aggadic* character and deals with issues of religious faith. It teaches you how the great lawyers of the Talmud are also important theologians, people who work out religious beliefs in a systematic and responsible way.

When you have studied these four passages, you will not know much Talmud. But you should have a clear picture of what the Talmud is and how it works. You may even want to learn more, not only *about* the Talmud but *in* the Talmud itself. If you do, I should not be surprised.

The Talmud has kept the attention of the Jewish people for hundreds of years and not only because it is a holy book. You can revere a holy book, but you need not study and learn it. The Talmud has fascinated Jews because it is an interesting book.

Yet the point of interest in the Talmud is not the same as in the Mishnah. When we learn Mishnah, we find ourselves (not always, but often) in our own world. Mishnah is open to us. We can get at its ethical and religious issues because it is timeless. It mainly speaks of the ordinary world in which we live and tells us its ideals for and conceptions about that world. So we can move from a paragraph of the Mishnah to a happening in the world.

But while the Mishnah speaks of the world at large, the Talmud speaks of the Mishnah and, only indirectly, about the world in which we live and to which Mishnah speaks. So we have to ask questions not immediately relevant to our lives. But these questions—the meaning of Mishnah, the larger ideals of life contained in Scripture, the relationship of Mishnah to Scripture, for example—also impose upon our minds an experience of asking questions.

When we master Talmudic modes of learning, we acquaint our minds with a way of asking questions, a way of analyzing, a way of searching.

Mishnah speaks thoughtfully about the world. Talmud teaches us how to think about Mishnah—*and* about the world.

Mishnah searches out the reason and the order of the world. Talmud makes explicit the mode of reasonable thinking.

Mishnah is substance, Talmud is method. Mishnah is what we do and say. Talmud is how we think about what we do and say.

These generalizations are not the whole story. But they allow you to see immediately what I can and cannot promise.

I promise that everything before us will have a point and a purpose. All will make sense in context. I do maintain that what you will see in the Talmud is worth your vision and will shape and sharpen your vision. I do believe that what you will now encounter is interesting and important.

But that is what learning means: knowing something for the pleasure of knowing, not merely for the uses of knowledge. In this sense, learning Talmud is like learning something beautiful, even though it is not useful in any obvious way. It is studying something important and worth knowing, even though it is of no practical value.

I cannot promise that all the passages we will labor to understand will be immediately relevant to our own lives as is often true in the Mishnah. When we learn the Mishnah, we have to bring our questions to the Mishnah and try to relate the Mishnah's answers to our world.

We must learn the importance of using our minds in quest of beauty, love, truth, or holiness.

And the Talmud, which teaches us how to use our intelligence in a holy way, is worth our time and effort because knowing *how* it thinks and *what* it thinks is knowing something holy.

PART TWO

Talmudic Analysis of Halakhah

3. Assigning the Blame

MISHNAH BABA QAMMA 3:2

What makes the Talmud "Talmudic" is its power to see the complicated sides of a simple problem. Indeed, the more Talmud you learn, the more you realize that nothing is so simple as it seems. For instance, if you slip on the ice in front of someone's house, you naturally blame the person who owns the house and who is responsible to sand the sidewalk. But what if the owner went to Arizona for the winter and hired a man to clean the walk and sand it? Who is responsible now—the owner or the man he hired?

And what if the contractor did hire a worker, and the worker did spread what he thought was sand, but the sand did no good—because it was not what it seemed? Then is not the person who sold the faulty sand to blame? But he bought the material from someone else, who made it—and so it goes. Nothing is what it appears to be at the outset.

The issue of placing blame is serious because once a person bears the blame or responsibility for something, he or she has to pay for the damages that have been caused. We all want to place the blame on the next person whenever something does go wrong, and chances are we have a considerable job to think through who should have prevented the accident.

Where does the accident take place? That is yet another thing to consider. What you do in your own property and what you do in a public park or on a public road are not the same. You may use what is yours. But may you do the same thing in an area that belongs to everyone equally? You may pick your own flowers but not the flowers in a park. You may leave your garage in a mess, but you may not mess up a baseball field.

Put these two things together now:

1. You have to fix the blame.

2. What you do in private property you may not do in public property.

That brings us to the problem of our first Mishnah. It presents three separate actions. First, someone puts out into the public road a pile of thorns or glass. Or, second, he or she makes a fence out of thorns or glass. Or, third, he or she builds a fence on his or her own property, but the fence falls into the sidewalk or road. Other people are hurt, stumbling onto the glass, scratching themselves against the fence, or falling over the fence that is in the roadway. The one who has done these things is liable to pay damages to the injured person. Here is the Mishnah-passage.

1	He who puts out thorn(s) and glass	הַמַּצְנִיעַ אֶת הַקּוֹץ וְאֶת הַזְּכוּכִית
2	and he who makes his fence of thorns	וְהַגּוֹדֵר אֶת גְּדֵרוֹ בְּקוֹצִים
3	and a fence which fell into the public way	וְנָדֵר שֶׁנָּפַל לִרְשׁוּת הָרַבִּים
4	and other people are hurt by them	וְהֻזְּקוּ בָהֶן אֲחֵרִים --
5	he is liable for their injury.	חַיָּב בְּנִזְקוֹ.

Vocabulary

put out, hide	מַצְנִיעַ	public way	רְשׁוּת הָרַבִּים
thorn	קוֹץ	is injured	הֻזַּק
glass	זְכוּכִית	liable	חַיָּב
builds a fence	גוֹדֵר	injury	נֶזֶק
fell	נָפַל		

The meaning of the Mishnah-passage is not obvious. We have to ask, "What does it tell us? And what are the kinds of questions that it does not answer?" For these kinds of questions are the ones that the Talmud must raise. How far does the Mishnah-passage go in unfolding its problem? And what is left for the Talmud to do? We shall ask these questions each time we learn a Mishnah-passage.

Now the point of No. 1 and No. 3 is clear: a person has taken over the public road for his or her private needs. Someone else is hurt because of what this person has done. But why should a person who builds a fence on his or her own property be liable for damages caused to someone who is scratched by it? After all, the owner of the fence has done no wrong. That seems like a fair question to address to this Mishnah-passage.

Now there is another sort of thinking we must learn how to do: how to take a principle and apply it to a fresh problem. For example: we know that if a person puts thorns or glass in the public road, he or she has to pay damages to anyone injured thereby. But what if a person tears down the wall not knowing there are thorns and glass in it, and thorns and glass fall into the road? Who is responsible—the owner of the wall? or the person who put the thorns and glass into the wall?

The owner did not put the thorns or glass into the wall. The owner has done nothing to cause damage. But the one who did put the thorns and glass into the wall did *not* tear down the wall and spread the thorns and glass onto the road. So this is a new problem, yet it comes out of the old one.

Once we know that the owner is responsible, we must ask about things for which the owner is not *directly* but still is *ultimately* responsible. That matter of ultimate, or second-level, responsibility is not to be missed.

There is still another level of meaning. We have to keep the law. But we want to do more than that. Some people do only what they must. But good people do more. Some people *avoid causing* accidents on their own. Others act in a positive way to *prevent* accidents. Some people drive too fast and only slow down when they see a police car. Others drive at safe speeds all the time. Obviously, no one is *always* virtuous, and no one is *never* virtuous. Most of us fall in the middle. But what do the most virtuous people do? That is something we are going to want to know.

Clearly the work of the explanation of our Mishnah-passage is going to be considerable. We have three areas of concern. First, we want to know why the person referred to in No. 2 is responsible for damage caused by a fence the person built on his or her own property. Second, we want to know about complications in Nos. 1 and 3, when one person does not do the damage, yet is still ultimately responsible for it. Third, we have a question about what we *should* do—not only what we must *not* do—to avoid hurting other people.

20

4.
Explaining the Mishnah

I f you look again at our passage of Mishnah, the first thing you notice is the problem in No. 2: Why should someone be liable merely for building a wall of thorns on his or her own property? People do have the right to build on their own land whatever they want. If outsiders stumble onto their land and get hurt, that is not the fault of the land-owner, who did not invite or expect the outsider.

One of the earlier Amoraim, Yohanan, will now answer that question. What he will do is simple and daring. He will impose an idea of his own upon the Mishnah. This he does by defining the *case* to which Mishnah refers. By saying what case the Mishnah treats, he excludes many cases from the rule of Mishnah. And by limiting the case to which Mishnah applies, he greatly changes the meaning that Mishnah had to begin with.

The first five lines (A-E) contain Yohanan's comment on the Mishnah-passage. The next three (F-H) have a further explanation of what Yohanan has said.

A. Said R. Yohanan, | א״ר (אָמַר רַבִּי) יוֹחָנָן

B. This Mishnaic ruling refers only | לֹא שָׁנוּ אֶלָּא

C. [to a case in which thorns] projected. | מַפְרִיחַ

D. But [in a case in which they were] confined [to private property], | אֲבָל מְצַמְצֵם

E. there is no liability [he is exempt]. | לֹא

F. Why is he exempt [in this case]? | מ״ט (מַאי טַעֲמָא) פָּטוּר?

G. Said R. Aha son of R. Iqa,

H. Because it is not the way of people to rub against walls.

אָמַר רַב אַחָא בְּרֵיהּ דְּרַב אִיקָא

לְפִי שֶׁאֵין דַּרְכָּן שֶׁל בְּנֵי אָדָם לְהִתְחַכֵּךְ בַּכְּתָלִים.

Vocabulary

they taught	שָׁנוּ
project	מַפְרִיחַ
be confined	מְצַמְצֵם
what is the reason?	מ״ט (מַאי טַעֲמָא)
the way of people	דַּרְכָּן שֶׁל בְּנֵי אָדָם
to rub against	לְהִתְחַכֵּךְ
walls	כְּתָלִים

Yohanan asks the obvious question: "Why should the fence I build on my own property cause me to be blamed if someone is injured by it? After all, what's on my land is mine. If you don't want to get hurt, keep off my land."

Yohanan takes Mishnah No. 2 and turns it on its head. He does so by reading into Mishnah precisely the concern we have spelled out. According to Yohanan, the Mishnaic ruling refers only to a fence of thorns *when the thorns project out onto the public road.* But if the thorns do not project onto the public road, and someone is injured by them, the owner of the fence pays nothing.

Is Yohanan reading something into our Mishnah-passage? Or has he some basis for what he says in what Mishnah says for itself? I am inclined to think he is on strong ground. For look at Mishnah No. 1: He who *puts out* thorns and glass. We took for granted that this means, He who puts out *onto the public road.*

22

No. 3 clinches the matter: a fence that fell into the public way. The context, therefore, says precisely what Yohanan claims phrase No. 2 also says. The whole Mishnah-passage speaks of damage done in the public way. Why should Yohanan not claim that our clause also addresses that same circumstance?

We still must explain why a person would not be liable for damages caused on his or her own property. After all, in general one has to be careful, even at home, not to injure other people. This question is what Aha, son of Iqa, wants to answer.

I might be responsible for what happens on my own land if I could foresee that it might happen. That is, if I have a big hole on my property and someone falls into it, there are circumstances in which I shall be held to blame. But if people in general are not likely to hurt themselves, how could I foresee that this particular person would be injured?

This is the view of Aha. If I maintain a nuisance on my own property, I might be liable. But if people do not usually injure themselves in the way in which this person has been injured, there is no way that I could foresee what has happened. I could not, therefore, have prevented this accident. I do not have to pay.

People generally do not rub themselves up against walls. How could I know that this person would do what no normal person does? The injured party is to blame. I should not have to pay. And I do not have to pay. Aha completes the statement begun by Yohanan. Yohanan has specified the circumstance in which I *am* responsible. Aha has explained the circumstance in which I am *not* responsible.

Have the Amoraim before us, Yohanan and Aha b. R. Iqa, fully explained the Mishnah-passage? The answer to that question depends on you. If you can think of questions they have not asked, or of situations for which they have not made a ruling, then you will have to join in the discussion begun by Yohanan and Aha.

5. Expanding the Mishnah's Rule

Our Mishnah-passage raises its own questions. We know that a person is responsible for what he or she does. If I cause damage and am liable to pay, I pay. But what happens if I do not cause the damage directly? What if someone else starts that chain of events that ends with my doing harm to someone else?

Let us take the case begun in our Mishnah-passage. I cannot put away thorns and glass by dumping them into the road. But my neighbor, who is building a fence, can use these materials. Without telling him, I go and pour my garbage—my thorns and glass—into the fence. Then as the fence is built up, the thorns and glass are covered over. Have I done right? Surely I have.

Then what happens? The owner of the fence tears it down because he or she wants to open his field. As a result, glass I hid in the fence is now poured into the public way. Someone is cut on the glass I put in the fence. Am I responsible? Is the owner of the fence responsible? Mishnah as we know it does not answer this question. Why not? Because Yohanan has only told me that if my glass and thorns are made into a fence on private property, I do not have to pay.

Well, I did put them into a fence on private property. Someone else has made them fall into the road. But why should that other person—the owner of the fence—be made to pay? After all, the glass and thorns belong to me.

This is the problem of the following teaching (A-E). Section A uses a formula that you will see again, *Our rabbis have taught.* The word for taught, תנה , means "repeat." The meaning is that this is a tradition that goes along with Mishnah's teachings. The language is the same as that of Mishnah in general. So is the way in which the words are arranged, as you will notice if you compare the sentence-pattern of the passage before us (called a *"baraita"*) with the Mishnah's sentence-pattern.

After A, our *baraita* proceeds to give its rule, and, once more, we have Yohanan's comment on it.

24

A. Our rabbis have taught:

תָּ"ר (תָּנוּ רַבָּנָן)

B. a person who hid thorns and broken glass in the wall of his fellow,

הַמַּצְנִיעַ קוֹצוֹתָיו וּזְכוּכִיּוֹתָיו לְתוֹךְ כּוֹתֶל שֶׁל חֲבֵירוֹ

C. and the owner of the wall came and tore down his wall,

וּבָא בַּעַל כּוֹתֶל וְסָתַר כּוֹתְלוֹ,

D. and it [the thorns or glass] fell into the public road and did damage—

וְנָפַל לרה"ר (לִרְשׁוּת הָרַבִּים) וְהִזִּיקוּ,

E. the one who hid [them in the wall] is liable.

חַיָּיב הַמַּצְנִיעַ.

F. Said R. Yohanan,

א"ר יוֹחָנָן

G. This teaching refers only to a wobbly wall.

לֹא שָׁנוּ אֶלָּא בְּכוֹתֶל רָעוּעַ,

H. But in the case of a solid wall,

אֲבָל בְּכוֹתֶל בָּרִיא

I. he who hides [them] away is exempt,

הַמַּצְנִיעַ פָּטוּר,

J. but liable is the owner of the wall [who tore it down].

וְחַיָּיב בַּעַל הַכּוֹתֶל.

Vocabulary

his thorns	קוֹצוֹתָיו
his broken glass	זְכוּכִיּוֹתָיו
wall	כּוֹתֶל
tore down	סָתַר
fell down	נָפַל
the public road	רה"ד (רְשׁוּת הָרַבִּים)
did damage	הִזִּיקוּ
wobbly	רָעוּעַ
solid	בָּרִיא

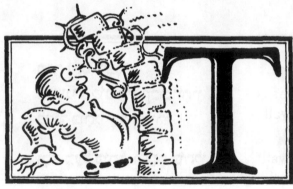

he question of responsibility is answered simply: the person who put the thorns and glass into the wall is responsible when the thorns and the glass pour out of the wall and onto the public road. The one who *ultimately* causes the injury is the one who pays. The owner of the wall owes nothing. Why not? Because he or she did not put the glass and thorns into the wall to begin with.

Yohanan (F-J) is not very happy with this one-sided ruling. Why should the owner of the wall bear no responsibility? After all, this owner tore down the wall and caused the carefully placed thorns and glass to scatter onto the public road.

Yohanan's solution is to rewrite the *baraita,* just as he rewrote the Mishnah-passage.

He says that the one who hid the thorns and glass in the wall bears full responsibility only when the wall is not a strong one. If it is wobbly and obviously going to collapse, then this is hardly a safe place for the thorns and glass. The one who puts them there has to have the foresight to expect the wall to collapse and the thorns and glass to fall out onto the public road. So what happens is his or her fault.

But if the wall is solid, then the one who hid thorns and glass in its rubble has no reason whatsoever to expect the thorns and glass to end up on the highway. The person did the right thing, in the right way. So, Yohanan maintains, the one who tears down the wall is responsible for whatever happens.

Why? Because the owner of the wall must take responsibility for rubble caused by tearing down the (formerly solid) wall. And so he or she must put away the thorns and glass that—after all—helped to build the wall to begin with.

Yohanan's distinction between a wobbly wall and a solid wall thus allows him to turn around the sense and meaning of the *baraita.* Now we cannot turn to the context of the *baraita* to ask whether the person who made it up would concur with Yohanan. But do you think he would? I doubt

26

it because the author of the *baraita* knows no distinctions between one kind of wall and another.

The author of the *baraita* is clear on his view. The person who puts thorns or glass into the wall is responsible for what they do if and when they fall out of the wall. That person has not done his or her job. So you must take careful measures, even beyond the requirements of the law, in order to avoid doing harm to other people. That is the opinion of the pious rabbis of the Talmud whom we shall meet in the next chapter.

Yohanan is a brave man. Living a long time after the completion of Mishnah, he is willing to take a critical view of the ideas and rules of Mishnah. He is happy to say what he thinks. He does this by discovering in Mishnah's words the ideas he holds and the conceptions that he has formed of what is right and just. He then has the courage to insist that the *baraita*, too, claims what he believes Mishnah says. And why not—since if he is right about the Mishnah-passage and its meaning, he must also be correct about the *baraita* and its message.

6. Explaining the Expansion

We have spoken thus far only about the specific case of our Mishnah-passage. We have a fence, glass, thorns, and a public road. Are we limited to this case? Or will the principle extend to a variety of cases? Obviously, no rule can state all the possible applications. We must be able to take the rule and find its general principle, then apply that general principle to a wide variety of cases. Otherwise we are stuck with useless facts.

If all we talk about is one event or one situation, then we don't have laws at all. When each event is treated differently from all others, then there are no rules. When there are no rules, there can be no justice. How can things be done fairly, if there is one law for me and a different law for you? We have to be under one and the same rule for fair play to be possible. Now the expansion of the Mishnah-passage accomplished (1) by the *baraita* and (2) by Yohanan, respectively, calls forth its own explanation and expansion. Rabina, who lived more than a hundred years after Yohanan, will give us a fresh case.

But the case only looks new. In fact, it would appear to say something so obvious as not to require saying. If we know the rule that governs the wall, we will not need a new case to repeat that old principle.

So the problem of explaining the expansion of the Mishnah-passage is this. We must make sense of what appears to be not an explanation, but merely a repetition. Why say the same thing twice? The passage before us begins with a second version of the story of the wall (A-D). Then we shall be told that the version is obvious. Then (E-I) the real purpose will be accomplished, that is, to say something new and interesting.

A. Said Rabina,	אָמַר רָבִינָא
B. That is to say, He who covers his pit with the cover of his fellow,	זֹאת אוֹמֶרֶת הַמְכַסֶּה בּוֹרוֹ בְּדַלְיוֹ שֶׁל חֲבֵירוֹ
C. and the owner of the cover	וּבָא בַּעַל דְּלִי

28

came along and took away his cover—

וְנָטַל דְּלִיו -

D. the owner of the pit is liable [for damage done to someone who falls into the pit].

חַיָּיב בַּעַל הַבּוֹר.

E. That is obvious!

פְּשִׁיטָא

F. What might you have said [had you not been told the case about the pit]?

מַהוּ דְּתֵימָא.

G. [You might have said], this ruling [about the wall] applies where [the owner of the wall] did not know [the identity of the one who put thorns or glass into his wall] so as to inform him [that he planned to tear it down].

הָתָם הוּא
דְּלָא הֲוִי יָדַע לֵיהּ
לְלוֹדָעֵיהּ.

H. But here [in the case of the pit], where he [the owner of the cover] knew [the identity of the one who had borrowed his cover to cover up the pit], he should have informed him [of his plan to remove the cover] [and therefore the owner of the cover is liable].

אֲבָל הָכָא
דְּיָדַע לֵיהּ
הֲוָה לֵיהּ לְאוֹדוֹעֵיהּ.

I. Thus the ruling teaches us [that the contrary is the case. That is, the owner of the pit remains responsible under all circumstances].

קמ״ל (קָא מַשְׁמַע לָן).

Vocabulary

one who covers [something]   הַמְכַסֶּה

pit	פּוֹר
cover	דְּלִי
took away	נָטַל
That is obvious!	פְּשִׁיטָא
What might you have said?	מַהוּ דְּתֵימָא
there	הָתָם
know [the identity of]	יָדַע
to inform	לוֹדִיעַ
here	הָכָא
he should have informed him	הֲוָה לֵיהּ לְאוֹדוֹעֵיהּ
the ruling teaches us	קמ״ל (קָא מַשְׁמַע לָן)

irst comes the case, then the analysis. The case is simple. I have a pit on my land. I need to cover it up. My neighbor has a garbage can with a lid. I take the lid and use it to cover over the hole in my ground. The neighbor comes over and takes the lid back. Then someone walks on my land and falls into the hole. Does my neighbor have to pay? Obviously not! He or she did not dig the hole and was not responsible to cover it. I dug the hole. I did not cover it properly. I am responsible.

Now did I tell you anything you did not know?

Not if you paid attention to the *baraita* we just studied. For if I put thorns or glass into a wobbly wall, I am responsible for damage that they do. Why? Because I have to suppose the wall may fall down. If I cover a hole with a lid belonging to my neighbor, I am responsible for damages done by the hole. Why? Because I have to realize my neighbor is going to need the lid back.

Rabina is not going to say obvious things. Therefore, he must have told this case for a reason. And he also has to know the story of the wobbly wall.

So what can be his purpose?

30

That is the view of E and F: What seems obvious is not, when you realize what you might have imagined!

G and H show what is at issue. They read into the *baraita* a problem and a solution just as Yohanan, when he read the *baraita*, rephrased its message. This is, as I said, a free and courageous process in which people use their minds and exercise their reason without restraint.

The *baraita* tells of a wall owner who is in no way responsible for what the wobbly wall has done. The one who put the glass and thorns in the wall should have had the foresight to realize the wobbly wall would fall.

But, if the wall owner told the owner of the glass and thorns of what was going to happen, the owner of the glass and thorns would be responsible.

If the owner of the wall did *not* inform the owner of the glass and thorns, who is responsible? Surely not the owner of the glass and thorns! He or she never had a chance to correct the situation.

If the owner of the wall had told the person to take away the glass and thorns and the person did not do so then, *and only then,* will the owner of the thorns and glass bear the blame for damage done by them.

Now in the case of the pit, the owner of the cover knows who has taken the cover. The owner of the pit knows whose cover it is. What happens? C tells us that the owner of the cover comes along and takes it away. So [D], the owner of the pit is liable. Now this is a case in which the owner of the cover has a serious responsibility. He or she should have informed the man of the plan to take back the cover. So the owner of the pit should not be responsible.

Not so, not so! The owner of the pit is responsible under *all* circumstances. And if I did not know the case of the pit and the lid, I would never have been able to reach that necessary conclusion.

There is no duty to tell the one who owns the thorns, or the one who owns the pit, that those thorns or that pit will do injury to someone. The owner should know that. In both cases, therefore, the owner of the glass or the owner of the pit will bear full responsibility. The owner cannot shift the blame, or part of the blame, to someone else.

We have not gone far from our Mishnah-passage. We started by asking about who gets blamed. And we are still asking about who bears the blame. Only the details and the depth of our discussion have changed. The basic principle is the same; the basic conceptions are the same—and the essential rule is unchanged.

7. How the Pious People Do Things

How shall I behave so as not to cause injury to other people?

The Talmud's discussion of this question must come because we cannot be left only with a rule for the average person. We must know what the careful and conscientious person does. It is not enough, therefore, to be told why and how you will not be liable for damage done by your thorns and glass. You have to be told how to avoid doing damage, whether or not you will be liable.

The law is for ordinary folk. But we have to be told how the people who go beyond the strict requirement of the law conduct themselves. And that is the purpose of the *baraita* that follows. It too has a little explanation attached. The *baraita* is A-D, and E and F provide two illustrations. Then, to conclude this discussion, we have a reflection on the larger issue: How to learn to do not merely what the law requires, but what truly good people do.

A. Our rabbis have taught:	תָּ"ר
B. the pious men of old would hide away their thorns and pieces of glass in their fields,	חֲסִידִים הָרִאשׁוֹנִים הָיוּ מַצְנִיעִים קוֹצוֹתֵיהֶם וּזְכוּכְיוֹתֵיהֶם בְּתוֹךְ שָׂדוֹתֵיהֶן
C. and bury them three handbreadths deep.	וּמַעֲמִיקִים לָהֶן ג' טְפָחִים
D. so that the plough should not be hindered.	כְּדֵי שֶׁלֹּא יְעַכֵּב הַמַּחֲרֵישָׁה
E. R. Sheshet [who was blind] would throw them into the fire.	רַב שֵׁשֶׁת שָׁדֵי לְהוּ בְּנוּרָא.
F. Raba would throw them into the Tigris.	רָבָא שָׁדֵי לְהוּ בְּדִגְלַת
G. Said Rab Judah, Whoever wants to be pious	אָמַר רַב יְהוּדָה הַאי מָאן דְּבָעֵי לְמֶהֱוֵי חֲסִידָא

32

H. should carry out the teachings of the Division of Torts [avoiding causing damage to other people].

לְקַיֵּם מִילֵי דִנְזִיקִין

I. Raba said, [Such a person should observe] the teachings in Abot.

רָבָא אָמַר מִילֵי דְּאָבוֹת

J. And others say, The teachings of Berakhot.

וְאָמְרִי לָהּ, מִילֵי דִּבְרָכוֹת

Vocabulary

our rabbis have taught	תָּ"ר (תָּנוּ רַבָּנָן)
the pious men of old	חֲסִידִים הָרִאשׁוֹנִים
bury them	מַעֲמִיקִים
handbreadths	טְפָחִים
in order	כְּדֵי
be hindered	יְעַכֵּב
the plow	הַמַּחֲרִישָׁה
threw	שָׁדִי
fire	נוּרָא
the Tigris	דִּגְלַת
whoever wants to be	מַאן דְּבָעֵי לְמֶהֱוֵי
pious	חֲסִידָא
teachings	מִילֵי
the Division of Torts	נְזִיקִין
Abot	אָבוֹת
Berakhot	בְּרָכוֹת

he best way to avoid causing damage is to bury your thorns and glass away from the public road. They should be buried deep, so that the plough will not turn them up. When the thorns and glass are properly buried, then, but only then, you never have to worry about what will happen to them.

That ideal solution (B-D) is credited to the pious men of olden times. But then the Talmud refers to people of its own day, of the third and fourth centuries C.E. It shifts its language, as you might have noticed, from Hebrew, in which Mishnah-teachings and stories are told, to Aramaic, in which the Talmud's own authorities express their ideas. In E and F we have two examples of what living authorities do. Sheshet burns up the thorns and glass as best he can. He is blind and cannot rely on any other means of disposing of them. Raba throws them into the river that flows by his farm. This is a sure way of getting rid of them without danger to other people.

We notice, once more, how the Talmud respects the people of its own day. What the old authorities of Mishnah did is a great example of what pious people should do today. But we shall not ignore the pious people of our own day. Their deeds also are recorded. The attitude here is that we are not inferior to our fathers and mothers or to their fathers and mothers.

This brings us to the sayings that conclude our discussion.

They are unusual because they depart from the topic we have discussed and turn, instead, to the ethical principle underlying the topic and its rules. That principle is easy to state: We do not want to hurt other people. Rab Judah says that the purpose of being a religious person is to avoid hurting other people. That is why a person who wants to be truly religious should study the rules of Neziqin, that is, the fourth division of the Mishnah, the division that deals with torts and damages. Our Mishnah-passage is in that division. So what Judah is telling us is to study just what we have been studying.

Raba (I) and other people (J) have different views of what we need to know in order to be truly religious. Raba says a person should study the

34

teachings of Pirqe Abot. That is something we did in *Learn Mishnah* and will do later on, in the last pages of this book. J's message is that to be pious you have to know how to thank God for the good things God does for you. Therefore, you should study the teachings of Berakhot. We are going to study some of those teachings also.

8. The Talmud All Together

N ow that we have examined each unit of the larger Talmud, we have yet another task. It is to see as a whole the Talmud that serves our Mishnah-passage. And I want you to see the Talmud as it is printed. You will realize that while it looks like a mass of words—lacking all indication of where one sentence ends and another begins, one paragraph stops and another starts—you can in fact make out the complete thoughts and units of thought. You just need patience.

BABYLONIAN TALMUD BABA QAMMA 30A (EXCERPT)

I suggest that you read the passage out loud and explain it, phrase by phrase. Then read it a second time and explain it paragraph by paragraph. That is, give the main idea or gist of what the Talmud is saying as a single, complete idea. Then read it a third time and try to outline the way in which the Talmud organizes its ideas. The third time around, you should be able to predict what the Talmud is going to want to do when it confronts a particular passage of Mishnah.

The first time through, we shall read the passage along with its English translation so that you may review the meanings of each line at the same time that you are reading all of the lines in their sequence. The second time through, we shall read in Hebrew and in Aramaic, without the help of the English translation. If you are studying the book with a teacher, ask your teacher how the passage may be chanted, the way the true students of the Talmud sing out its words.

1	He who puts out thorns and glass	הַמַּצְנִיעַ אֶת הַקוֹץ וְאֶת הַזְּכוּכִית
2	and he who makes his fence of thorns	וְהַגּוֹדֵר אֶת גְּדֵרוֹ בַּקּוֹצִים
3	and a fence which fell into the public way	וְגָדֵר שֶׁנָּפַל לִרְשׁוּת הָרַבִּים

4	and other people are hurt by them	וְהוּזְקוּ בָהֶן אֲחֵרִים
5	he is liable for their injury.	חַיָּיב בְּנִזְקָן.

I.	A.	Said R. Yohanan,	א״ר (אָמַר רַבִּי) יוֹחָנָן,
	B.	This Mishnaic ruling refers only	לֹא שָׁנוּ אֶלָּא
	C.	[to a case in which thorns] projected.	מַפְרִיחַ,
	D.	But [in a case in which they were] confined [to private property],	אֲבָל מְצַמְצֵם
	E.	there is no liability [he is exempt].	לֹא.
	F.	Why is he exempt [in this case]?	מ״ט (מַאי טעמא) פָּטוּר?
	G.	Said R. Aha son of R. Iqa,	אָמַר רַב אַחָא בְּרֵיה דְרַב אִיקָא,
	H.	Because it is not the way of people to rub against the walls.	לְפִי שָׁאֵין דַּרְכָּן שֶׁל בְּנֵי אָדָם לְהִתְחַכֵּךְ בַּכְּתָלִים.
II.	A.	Our rabbis have taught:	ת״ר (תָּנוּ רַבָּנָן)
	B.	A person who hid thorns and broken glass in the wall of his fellow,	הַמַּצְנִיעַ קוֹצוֹתָיו וּזְכוּכִיוֹתָיו לְתוֹךְ כּוֹתָל שֶׁל חֲבֵירוֹ,
	C.	and the owner of the wall came and tore down his wall,	וּבָא בַּעַל כּוֹתָל וְסָתַר כּוֹתְלוֹ
	D.	and it [the thorns or glass] fell into the public road and did damage—	וְנָפַל לרה״ר (לִרְשׁוּת הָרַבִּים) וְהִזִּיקוּ,
	E.	the one who hid [them in the wall] is liable.	חַיָּיב הַמַּצְנִיעַ.
	F.	Said R. Yohanan,	א״ר יוֹחָנָן
	G.	This teaching refers only to a wobbly wall.	לֹא שָׁנוּ אֶלָּא בְּכוֹתָל רָעוּעַ,

H. But in the case of a solid wall,

I. he who hides [them] away is exempt,

J. but liable is the owner of the wall [who tore it down].

אָכַל בְּכוֹתָל בָּרִיא

הַמַּצְנִיעַ פָּטוּר,

וְחַיָּיב בַּעַל הַכּוֹתָל.

III. A. Said Rabina,

B. That is to say, He who covers his pit with the cover of his fellow,

C. and the owner of the cover came along and took away his cover—

D. the owner of the pit is liable [for damage done to someone who falls into the pit].

E. That is obvious!

F. What might you have said [had you not been told the case about the pit]?

G. [You might have said,] This ruling [about the wall] applies where [the owner of the wall] did not know [the identity of the one who put thorns or glass into his wall] so as to inform him [that he planned to tear it down].

H. But here [in the case of the pit], where he [the owner of the cover] knew [the identity of the one who had borrowed his cover to cover

אָמַר רָבִינָא

זֹאת אוֹמֶרֶת הַמְכַסֶּה בּוֹרוֹ בְּדַלְיוֹ שֶׁל חֲבֵירוֹ.

וּבָא בַּעַל דְּלִי וְנָטַל דַּלְיוֹ -

חַיָּיב בַּעַל הַבּוֹר.

פְּשִׁיטָא

מַהוּ דְּתֵימָא.

הָתָם הוּא דְּלָא הֲוֵי יָדַע לֵיהּ לְאוֹדְעֵיהּ.

אֲבָל הָכָא דְּיָדַע לֵיהּ הֲוָה לֵיהּ לְאוֹדוֹעֵיהּ.

38

up the pit], he should have informed him [of his plan to remove the cover] [and therefore the owner of the cover is liable].

I. Thus the ruling teaches us [that the contrary is the case. That is, the owner of the pit remains responsible under all circumstances].

קמ"ל (קָא מַשְׁמַע לָן).

IV. A. Our rabbis have taught:

ת"ר

B. the pious men of old would hide away their thorns and pieces of glass in their fields,

חֲסִידִים הָרִאשׁוֹנִים הָיוּ מַצְנִיעִים קוֹצוֹתֵיהֶם וּזְכוּכִיּוֹתֵיהֶם בְּתוֹךְ שְׂדוֹתֵיהֶן

C. and bury them three handbreadths deep,

וּמַעֲמִיקִים לָהֶן ג' טְפָחִים

D. so that the plough should not be hindered.

כְּדֵי שֶׁלֹּא יַעֲכֵב הַמַּחֲרֵישָׁה,

E. R. Sheshet [who was blind] would throw them into the fire.

רַב שֵׁשֶׁת שָׁדֵי לְהוּ בְּנוּרָא,

F. Raba would throw them into the Tigris.

רָבָא שָׁדֵי לְהוּ בְּדִגְלַת.

G. Said Rab Judah, Whoever wants to be pious

אָמַר רַב יְהוּדָה, הַאי מַאן דְּבָעֵי לְמֶהֱוֵי חֲסִידָא,

H. should carry out the teachings of the Division of Torts [avoiding causing damage to other people].

לְקַיֵּים מִילֵּי דִנְזִיקִין.

I. Raba said, [Such a person should observe] the teachings in Abot.

רָבָא אָמַר מִילֵּי דְאָבוֹת,

J. And others say, The teachings of Berakhot.

וְאָמְרִי לַהּ, מִילֵּי דִבְרָכוֹת

39

ow, as I said, let us look at the passage as it appears in the Talmud. Try to read it out loud—or better yet try to sing it.

המצניע את הקוץ ואת הזכוכית והגודר את גדרו בקוצים
וגדר שנפל לרשות הרבים והוזקו בהן אחרים חייב בנזקן

המצניע את הקוץ וכו׳]: א״ר יוחנן לא שנו אלא מפריח אבל
מצמצם לא מ״ט פטור אמר רב אחא בריה דרב איקא לפי שאין
דרכן של בני אדם להתחכך בכתלים ת״ר המצניע קוצותיו
וזכוכיותיו לתוך כותל של חבירו ובא בעל כותל וסתר כותלו ונפל
לרה״ר והוזקו המצניע חייב א״ר יוחנן לא שנו אלא בכותל רעוע
אבל בכותל בריא המצניע פטור וחייב בעל הכותל אמר רבינא
זאת אומרת המכסה בורו בדליו של חבירו ובא בעל דלי ונטל דליו
חייב בעל הבור פשיטא מהו דתימא התם הוא דלא הוי ידע ליה
דלודעיה אבל הכא דידע ליה הוה ליה לאודועיה קמ״ל ת״ר חסידים
הראשונים היו מצניעים קוצותיהם וזכוכיותיהם בתוך שדותיהן
ומעמיקים להן ג׳ טפחים כדי שלא יעכב המחרישה רב ששת שדי
להו בנורא רבא שדי להו בדגלת אמר רב יהודה האי מאן דבעי
למהוי חסידא לקיים מילי דנזיקין רבא אמר מילי דאבות ואמרי
לה מילי דברכות :

WHAT IS THE TALMUD?

A while ago we asked ourselves why the Mishnah needed the Talmud at all and what the Mishnah asks the Talmud to do. You have now studied an impor-

40

tant example of what the Talmud does for the Mishnah. Let us specify these important services to the Mishnah.

1. The Mishnah must be explained. There are various sides to the Mishnah that might require explanation. We may see an unusual word or phrase. We frequently (though not here) will ask about the Scriptural source for Mishnah's rule. In our passage Yohanan has been troubled by what he thought to be something unfair in Mishnah. Rather than spelling matters out in detail, our Talmudic passage has simply given Yohanan's conclusion. For our part, we used our reason to figure out what was bothering him and why he interpreted the Mishnah-passage as he did. This is done in Chapter 4.

2. The Mishnah's rule must be subjected to further thought. The work of Talmud is not merely to comment on Mishnah's language and its ideas. It has also to pay attention to the larger ideas that the Mishnah-passage implies. The second stage in the Talmud's work on Mishnah, therefore, is to separate the idea from the Mishnah-passage that expresses that idea. This we saw in Chapter 5.

3. Once we expand and explain Mishnah's rule, it is perfectly natural to go on and expand and explain our first expansion and explanation. For sometimes what we think is expansion is simply repetition. And the Talmud does not respect people who merely repeat themselves or say in other words what someone already has clearly said. So if the Talmud contains another version of a saying or a story or a rule, and if it then chooses to cite and quote that other version, the first thing the Talmud will ask is, "Is all this not perfectly obvious? If it is obvious, then why are you telling it to me?" This is the exercise of Chapter 6.

4. If the Talmud were interested only in ordinary folk, its discussion of the present Mishnah-passage would have come to an end at Chapter 6. But the Talmud wants to present us with more than *rules* for everyday people. The Talmud discusses *ideals* for which we can and should strive. That is why in the end it tells us what we should do to avoid having to know the rule with which we began. We can arrange if we want, to avoid causing damage, and we are able to cite the actual practice of religious people in this regard. This is the work of Chapter 7. At that same point in the unfolding of our unit of the Talmud, we have more general reflections. At that point our discussion is brought to a conclusion.

SO WHAT IS THE TALMUD?

Is it a "commentary"—an explanation—of the Mishnah? Of course it is, but it is more than that.

How much more?

Perhaps the obvious answer is, It is an expansion and extension of the Mishnah's rules.

But we already know that the Amoraim of our passage—Yohanan, Iqa, and others—move far beyond the rules of Mishnah. They will not hesitate to reverse what Mishnah says, to turn it right on its head.

So the Talmud's authorities are remarkably free and independent minds. They are deeply respectful of the Mishnah and its rules. But they are not enslaved by them. They take seriously what Mishnah has to tell them. But they also take to heart their own ideas.

So the Talmud is both dependent on and independent of the Mishnah.

It explains, expands, and spells out what the Mishnah says. But it also says what it wants to say.

TALMUD, TORAH, JUDAISM

Now that you have completed your first exercise in learning Talmud, you should not forget why you began this work. It was because Talmud is part of Torah, and Torah is the same as Judaism. Torah is the word we use at home when to the world outside we use the word Judaism. Just as we ask, "What is Talmud?" it is fair to ask, "What have we learned about Torah, that is, about Judaism?"

One small passage of the Talmud obviously does not provide the whole answer. But surely part of a whole answer is to say, "Judaism is a religion about a wobbly wall." Judaism speaks about concrete questions of how to act in ordinary life. One important concern of Judaism is to make us people who accept and carry out our responsibilities to other people. To drive a car so as to endanger the life of someone else is a sin in Judaism. To build a wall that is firm and prevents people from getting hurt is a good deed.

The Talmud is important for Judaism today not because it was important a long time ago, but because it teaches us to think about the world in which we live.

PART THREE

A Complete Passage of Talmud

9.
I Didn't Really Mean It

MISHNAH NEDARIM 9:1-2

The Talmud has more to say about the Mishnah-passage that we just studied; we only considered an excerpt. This was helpful in showing us how the Talmud does its business. But it does not give us a clear picture of how the Talmud completely discusses a given Mishnah-passage. For this purpose we turn now to one of the most interesting kinds of Mishnah-law, which has to do with the force of the words we say.

In the times of the Mishnah and the Talmud, people believed that if they took a vow, they had to keep it. If they did not keep it, they feared that Heaven would punish them. For example, someone might say something in a fit of anger. Afterward he would not dismiss as nothing what he had said. He would be full of remorse. He would do what he had said he would do.

This sort of vow might be as follows in our day. You are arguing with your friend. You get so angry at him or her that you say, "I'll never talk to you again." Ten minutes later you get over the argument. But you've said something. Now how do you take it back? In olden times, things were not much different. You have a friend who wants you to come to his or her house for dinner. You don't want to go. In order to persuade this person to stop nagging you, you shout, "*Qonam* be anything I eat of yours." "Qonam" is a word that imitates the word *Qorban*, offering or sacrifice. What you have said, therefore, is that as far as you are concerned, any of your friend's food is equivalent to a sacrifice in the Temple. That means you cannot eat such food. For you cannot eat the animal-sacrifices that are offered up to God or reserved for the Temple priests. It follows that your friend had better stop nagging you because you are not in a position to eat this food again.

This sort of "vowing" took place among ordinary folk because they would frequently lose their tempers and explode into vows. Since they believed that God hears what human beings say, just as God oversees what human beings do, they knew they had to keep their word. And they most certainly did keep their vows.

But that is only part of the story. The sages of the Mishnah and the Talmud understood that circumstances can change. A person might take a vow and not really mean it. For example, if you are arguing with someone and you said, "*Qonam* be my chair if I did not see the Boston Red Sox play twenty times more than you ever did," that would just be an exaggeration. The rabbis of the Mishnah understand that that is not really a vow. It is just a statement you happen to throw at someone else.

What happens, however, if matters are not so clear? It is possible that there can be a valid vow, which in the end can be released or untied. We should say "untie" and "tie up" a vow because a vow ties you up in knots— knots made of words. Sages are able to untie the knots of vows if they can find suitable grounds. They are able to show that the vow you made was never binding; it never did tie you up in knots at all. You thought it did, and you kept it. But a sage can find the grounds to declare otherwise.

The Mishnah-passage before us asks, "What are acceptable grounds for declaring a vow to be null?" Eliezer has an interesting idea. He points out that only gross people take vows. It is a sign that you are not well brought up, that you do not think before you speak, that you do not have your wits about you. So, he says, we should declare as proper grounds for untying a vow the fact that by taking the vow, the person has brought shame to his or her father and mother. People will go around saying, "Mr. and Mrs. So-and-so have raised a loud-mouth bum."

So the sage should ask the fellow, "If you had known that people would go around and speak ill of your parents, would you have taken your vow?"

If the man says, "No, I should never have vowed had I known people would make fun of my parents for having me as their son," that is enough.

The vow is untied.

Sages reject this opinion. They do not think that is a sufficient reason to untie the vow.

Then Sadoq comments rather sarcastically on Eliezer's idea. He points out that vows bring shame not only to one's father and mother. They also bring shame to God.

After all, taking such vows is hardly respectful to Heaven. And, he then says, if such were to be suitable grounds for untying the vow, then no vow would be valid. For under all and any circumstances, someone could readily say, "If I had known that by taking this dumb vow, I should bring disgrace to Heaven, I should never have taken that vow."

So, Sadoq says, Eliezer's position leads to the absurd result that there never could be a valid vow.

Finally, sages concede one thing to Eliezer. They say that if a person took a vow that affects one's relations with one's parents—for example, refusing to visit them ever—then you can untie the vow by saying something about the honor you owe your father and mother.

If a daughter, for instance, took a vow not to visit her father and mother, you can say to her, "If you had known that by taking this vow, you could not pay respect to your father and mother, would you have taken the vow?" If the girl says, "No," then you have the power to declare the vow untied.

This is not granting much to Eliezer, for the girl has taken a vow contrary to what the Torah requires, which is that she honor her father and her mother. Sadoq will not be offended by sages' concession. Why not? Because, so far as he is concerned, this is a minor matter—as opposed to the world-shaking conception that vows may be untied by reference to the honor of God.

Let us now turn to the first part of the Mishnah-passage to which the Talmud we shall study is devoted.

---

1 Rabbi Eliezer says:

They untie [a vow] for a person on account of the honor of his father and his mother.

And sages prohibit [keep it tied].

רַבִּי אֱלִיעֶזֶר אוֹמֵר:
פּוֹתְחִין לָאָדָם בִּכְבוֹד אָבִיו וְאִמּוֹ;
וַחֲכָמִים אוֹסְרִין.

2 Said Rabbi Sadoq:

Before they untie [a vow] for him on account of his father and his mother, let them untie it for him on account of the honor of the Omnipresent.

[And] if so, there will be no vows [at all]!

אָמַר רַבִּי צָדוֹק:
עַד שֶׁפּוֹתְחִין לוֹ בִּכְבוֹד
אָבִיו וְאִמּוֹ, יִפְתְּחוּ לוֹ
בִּכְבוֹד הַמָּקוֹם,
אִם כֵּן אֵין נְדָרִים!

46

3   And sages agree with Rabbi Eliezer concerning a matter [about which he vowed] between his father and his mother, that they untie it for him on account of the honor of his father and his mother.

וּמוֹדִים חֲכָמִים לְרַבִּי אֱלִיעֶזֶר בְּדָבָר שֶׁבֵּינוֹ לְבֵין אָבִיו וְאִמּוֹ, שֶׁפּוֹתְחִין לוֹ בִּכְבוֹד אָבִיו וְאִמּוֹ.

Vocabulary

untie	פּוֹתְחִין	before	עַד
man	אָדָם	if	אִם
with honor	בִּכְבוֹד	so	כֵּן
his father	אָבִיו	the Lord	הַמָּקוֹם
his mother	אִמּוֹ	vows	נְדָרִים
sages	חֲכָמִים	agree	מוֹדִים
forbid	אוֹסְרִין	between	בֵּין

The next part of the Mishnah-passage is much easier to follow because it explains itself. As you will see if you look at the passage rapidly, Nos. 5, 6, and 7 give examples of the same point as is made in No. 4. Eliezer's position is that if something happens after you take a vow, you can say, "If I had known that that would happen, I should never have vowed." As a result, your vow is null. Sages declare that what happens after the vow has no effect upon the vow. Why not? Because you take the vow in full knowledge of what you are saying. If you are wrong, it is a vow made in error. You are not bound by such a vow. But if the facts are what you think they are, then there are no grounds to untie the vow. It was valid and remains in force. The right grounds for annulling a vow must be that things were not what you thought they were when you said what you said. Then you can claim "There never really was a vow in force."

4	And furthermore did Rabbi Eliezer say:	וְעוֹד אָמַר רַבִּי אֱלִיעֶזֶר:
	They untie [a vow] on account of something which happened [later on]	פּוֹתְחִין בְּנוֹלָד;
	And sages prohibit	וַחֲכָמִים אוֹסְרִין.
5	How so?	כֵּיצַד?
	[If] he said, *Qonam*—that I shall not derive benefit from so-and-so	אָמַר: קוֹנָם שֶׁאֵינִי נֶהֱנֶה לְאִישׁ פְּלוֹנִי,
	and he [so-and-so] became a scribe	וְנַעֲשָׂה סוֹפֵר,
	or was going to marry off his son very soon	אוֹ שֶׁהָיָה מַשִּׂיא אֶת בְּנוֹ בְּקָרוֹב,
6	and he said, If I had known that he would become a scribe	וְאָמַר: אִלּוּ הָיִיתִי יוֹדֵעַ שֶׁהוּא נַעֲשָׂה סוֹפֵר,
	or that he would marry off his son very soon	אוֹ שֶׁהוּא מַשִּׂיא אֶת בְּנוֹ בְּקָרוֹב-
	I should not have taken a vow	לֹא הָיִיתִי נוֹדֵר.
7	*Qonam* against this house, that I shall not enter it and it was made into a synagogue	קוֹנָם לְבַיִת זֶה שֶׁאֵינִי נִכְנָס, וְנַעֲשָׂה בֵּית הַכְּנֶסֶת,
	[if] he said, If I had known that it would be made into a synagogue, I should not have taken a vow	אָמַר: אִלּוּ הָיִיתִי יוֹדֵעַ שֶׁהוּא נַעֲשָׂה בֵּית הַכְּנֶסֶת, לֹא הָיִיתִי נוֹדֵר-
8	Rabbi Eliezer unties [the vow]	רַבִּי אֱלִיעֶזֶר מַתִּיר;
	And sages prohibit [keep it tied].	וַחֲכָמִים אוֹסְרִין.

Vocabulary

unexpected event	נוֹלָד	marry	מַשִּׂיא
how	כֵּיצַד	soon	בְּקָרוֹב
benefit	נֶהֱנָה	if	אִלּוּ
person	אִישׁ	know	יוֹדֵעַ
such-and-such	פְּלוֹנִי	enter	נִכְנָס
became	נַעֲשָׂה	synagogue	בֵּית כְּנֶסֶת
scribe	סוֹפֵר	permits	מַתִּיר

The cases provide a beautiful explanation for the basic dispute. We have three examples of precisely the same thing. In each of them (5, 6, and 7), a person says that if he or she had known what was going to happen later on, he or she would not have taken such a vow. At the end (8) comes the predictable decision. Eliezer declares the vow to be untied. These are suitable grounds because they untie a vow on account of something which happens later on. Sages declare the vow to be tied. These are not suitable grounds. The vow was valid when the person took it. Why should it not be valid now?

10. Explaining the Mishnah

The most interesting statement in the Mishnah-passage we just examined is the claim of Sadoq that if we agree with Eliezer, there won't be any more vows.

Precisely what does he mean?

Does he mean that no one will vow any more? Why should that be the case merely because we have made it remarkably easy to untie a vow? Sadoq claims that if we may untie a vow on the grounds that a vow is not respectful to God, there will not be any more vows at all. This is a curious statement.

The first task of the Talmud that serves our Mishnah-passage is to explain the meaning of the language. As soon as that work is done, we immediately test the meaning we have assigned to the Mishnah-passage. We have to be sure that we are right. And this we shall do by reading the rest of the Mishnah-passage in the light of the explanations we have given.

First, let us examine the meaning of Sadoq's saying as it is analyzed by the great Amoraim, Abbaye and Raba.

A. What is [the meaning of,] "There will be no vows?	מַאי אֵין נְדָרִים?
B. Said Abbaye,	אֲמַר אַבַּיֵי
C. If so, no vows may be unbound.	אִם כֵּן אֵין נְדָרִים נִיתָּרִין יָפֶה.
D. And Raba said,	וְרָבָא אֲמַר
E. If so, Vows will not be brought for inquiry [and absolution] to a sage.	א"כ (אִם כֵּן) אֵין נְדָרִים נִשְׁאָלִין לְחָכָם.
F. We have learned:	תְּנָן
G. And sages concede to R. Eliezer that in a matter involving himself and his father and mother, they do	וּמוֹדִין חֲכָמִים לְרַבִּי אֱלִיעֶזֶר בְּדָבָר שֶׁבֵּינוֹ לְבֵין אָבִיו וְאִמּוֹ שֶׁפּוֹתְחִים לוֹ בִּכְבוֹד

release him by reason of the honor of his father and his mother.	אָבִיו וְאִמּוֹ.
H. Certainly, this accords with Abbaye, who said, If so, no vows may be unbound;	בִּשְׁלָמָא לְאַבַּיֵי דְּאָמַר אִם כֵּן אֵין נְדָרִים נִיתָּרִין
I. here, if he has been so impudent, he is impudent.	הָכָא כֵּיוָן דְּאִיחְצֵף לֵיהּ הָא אִיחְצֵף לֵיהּ.
J. But so far as Raba is concerned, who said, If so, vows will not be brought for inquiry [and absolution] to a sage,	אֶלָּא לְרָבָא דְּאָמַר אִם כֵּן אֵין נְדָרִים נִשְׁאָלִין לְחָכָם
K. in this case, why do they unbind [the vow]?	הָכָא אַמַּאי פּוֹתְחִין,
L. I shall tell you:	אַמְרֵי
M. since all vows cannot be [untied] without a sage,	כֵּיוָן דְּכָל נִדְרֵי לָא סַגְיָא לְהוֹן הֲלָאו חָכָם
N. here too they [sages] will declare the vow unbound.	הָכָא נַמִי פּוֹתְחִין.

Vocabulary

what	מַאי	here	הָכָא
unbound	נִיתָּרִין	he is impudent	אִיחְצֵף לֵיהּ
brought for inquiry	נִשְׁאָלִין	I shall tell you	אַמְרֵי
we have learned	תְּנָן	too	נַמִי
certainly	בִּשְׁלָמָא		

bbaye claims (B) that Sadoq means: If we accept the honor of God as a suitable pretext for annulling a vow, then there will be no more proper *annulling* of vows.

Abbaye's thinking is: On what grounds do we ever

51

declare a vow to be untied? It is because of genuine regret, when someone truly repents what he or she has said. If a person does not truly regret his or her vow, it cannot be properly annulled or untied. Now what happens if you say to someone, "Would you have taken such a vow if you had known it was not respectful to God?"

Is there anyone in the world who would have the gall—the *hutzpah*—to say, "Yes, I would have taken that vow!"?

Abbaye says, "No one in the world would make such a statement."

As a result, however, people will be able to untie vows that they do not sincerely repent taking. Why? Because no one is so impudent as to say otherwise. As a result, vows will no longer be properly revoked.

In other words, the grounds for untying the vow, in Sadoq's opinion, are so slight that vows that still should be binding will be untied.

That is one way of seeing Sadoq's statement in the Mishnah passage.

Raba's view is close to Abbaye's. But it still differs. Raba says, "You make it so easy to annul a vow that no one will go to a sage. Why not? Because everyone can do it for himself or herself."

God's honor applies to all vows. If it is sufficient grounds for annulling the vow, then everyone will carry out the untying without going to a sage. As a result, vows will no longer be supervised by sages.

Do Abbaye and Raba disagree?

According to what we have just said about their opinions, they certainly do not disagree. In fact, they say almost the same thing, though in slightly different language.

Each one is concerned about proper untying of vows. Abbaye is afraid that the wrong motives will be considered effective. Raba is afraid that the wrong people will do the untying. Both see Sadoq as expressing concern about the proper untying of vows by the right people for the right motive.

There is one small problem with Abbaye's and Raba's explanation of the Mishnah-passage.

Sadoq is not talking about *untying* vows. He is talking about *vows*.

He says to Eliezer that there will not be any more vows. He does not talk about proper untying of vows.

Yet Abbaye and Raba have a strong basis for what they read into Sadoq's sentence. It is this: Eliezer has spoken of grounds for *absolving*, not foundations for *making*, vows. So if we read what Sadoq has said as a reply to Eliezer, then it must have only one reference. Sadoq, too, must speak of untying vows, not making them. So when he says, "There will be no vows," he must mean, "There will be no untying of vows."

If that sentence in Sadoq's saying does not belong there, then it can be seen in a different way. It can mean bluntly and precisely what it says: "If it is so easy to annul vows, then no one will take vows any more, because vows will not be taken seriously.

What Sadoq means, viewed from this angle, is simple: If vows are easy to untie, then they will no longer be made: There will no longer be *valid* vows.

The Talmud proceeds to test what Abbaye and Raba offered as explanations of the Mishnah by placing their explanations up against the Mishnah-passage itself. This brings us to the quotation of No. 3 of the Mishnah-passage, which, you see, the Talmud cites word for word (F-G). The Talmud begins by saying, *We have learned*, which means, "we have learned in a Mishnah-passage." And it goes over the grounds that sages will accept for untying the vow.

Sages are willing to say that a vow is untied if a person confesses that he or she would not have taken such a vow had it been known that parents would be shamed.

If someone says, "If I had known what this would do to my father and mother, I should never have taken that vow," you can and should believe that person.

Why? Because someone possibly would say the contrary. Therefore, only if someone has honestly repented would he or she make such a claim.

As far as Abbaye is concerned, therefore, the vow is honestly and sincerely nullified by a statement concerning the honor of one's parents.

What about Raba?

He worried about people who would not go to a sage at all. If they won't go to a sage when the honor of God is involved, why should they go to a sage when the honor of their parents is involved? Will it follow that Raba cannot explain the concession of sages to Eliezer?

No, it will not follow.

Why not?

Because here, too, one will not be able to untie his or her own vow.

Why not? Because Raba makes it impossible for someone to untie a vow without a sage *in general*. He will make sure that it is general practice to go to a sage. In this case, too, therefore, people will go to a sage.

In other words, Abbaye distinguishes between the shame of parents and the shame of God. Raba holds that if you arrange things properly, then you will not have to worry about the case that sages concede.

Shall we then admit to Abbaye and Raba that what is important to them is important to the sages of Mishnah-passage No. 3? Is this the decisive consideration?

Not likely. For Raba and Abbaye explain the Mishnah-passage at one point and then proceed to explain the rest of the Mishnah-passage along the lines of that original explanation.

Is it then possible to explain better than Abbaye and Raba why sages will accept as suitable grounds for untying the vow the person's regret at shaming his or her parents? There certainly is a better reason.

Sages really concede nothing to Eliezer; they give up only a small point.

They say that if one takes a vow specifically involving a father or mother, and the vow shames the father or mother, one can go to a sage (as Raba wants) and claim that the vow would never have been taken had the person known how the vow would affect the father or mother. That is a far cry from saying, "Under all circumstances you can invoke the shame you have caused your family by being a person who takes vows!"

In fact, sages notice only that you can not take a vow that requires you to do something contrary to the law of the Torah. You can not take a vow that will require you to shame your father and your mother because we are all commanded to honor our fathers and our mothers.

If you have taken a vow that causes shame to come upon your father and your mother, that vow is null and void.

Why?

Because it contradicted the law of the Torah—and therefore never was valid, not at the outset, not at the end. So when the sage declares the vow to be untied, he says that it never was a vow.

That seems to me a more relevant explanation of the concession of the sages in No. 3 than reading the issues of No. 2 into the explanation of No. 3.

But can you find something even more persuasive?

The conversation continues. You can, and should, join in with Raba and Abbaye, Yohanan and Judah, and all the other great Amoraim. To be sure, you can join in only after you have listened to what they have to tell you.

11. The Sources of the Mishnah

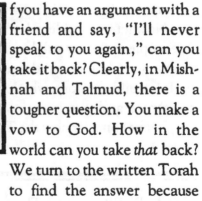

If you have an argument with a friend and say, "I'll never speak to you again," can you take it back? Clearly, in Mishnah and Talmud, there is a tougher question. You make a vow to God. How in the world can you take *that* back? We turn to the written Torah to find the answer because without its authority we simply have no right to untie what has been tied up in God's name. We also must find out how Eliezer can claim that a person may untie a vow on the basis of something that will happen long after the vow is made. Why should a later happening make any difference? Are there no rules? Is nothing sacred?

Eliezer makes an amazing assertion: you can declare a vow to be untied on the basis of something that happens after the vow is made. The position of sages seems reasonable. You declare untied a vow that never really was tied; it was null at the outset. Eliezer's opinion is daring. It also does not stand to reason, the way sages' view does. Therefore the Talmud must ask a basic question.

How does Eliezer know? What is the source of his opinion?

The only valid source, of course, is the Torah of Moses at Sinai, and, specifically, the written Torah.

When the Talmud asks for a source for what Mishnah holds, it is saying that Mishnah alone is not sufficient.

It implies that there is a superior, true source, which is the written Scripture, not the Mishnah.

If the question, "What is the source?" or, "What is the reason?" were addressed only to an individual rabbi of the Mishnah, you might come to a false conclusion. You might say that the Talmud asks for reasons and sources because it does not rely upon an individual. But if the Talmud faced an opinion in the name of all the sages—or in no one's name—then it would accept that opinion as Torah.

That is not true. The Talmud asks for the sources when the Mishnah speaks in the name of all of its authorities, just as often as when it quotes only one person's name. When the Talmud wants to know the Mishnah's authority, it is not satisfied with the authority of the Mishnah alone.

Now let us consider what will be a sufficient authority for the Mishnah. One ample authority will be a rule or a law given in Scripture in the name of Moses, our rabbi. But in the present case, we have another suitable authority. It is a biblical story, which indicates that the principle we are looking for is accepted and true.

Let us consider how the Talmud answers the question, What is Eliezer's reason?

A. R. Eliezer says, They unbind a vow on account of something that happened later on.

רַבִּי אֱלִיעֶזֶר פּוֹתְחִין בְּנוֹלָד כו׳

B. What is the reason of R. Eliezer?

מ״ט דְּרַבִּי אֱלִיעֶזֶר,

C. Said R. Hisda,

אָמַר רַב חִסְדָּא,

D. Since Scripture has said,

דְּאָמַר קְרָא:

E. [And the Lord said to Moses in Midian, Go, return to Egypt,] for all the men [who sought to kill you] are dead (Ex. 4:19).

כִּי מֵתוּ כָּל הָאֲנָשִׁים,

F. Now death was something that happened later on.

וְהָא מִיתָה דְּנוֹלָד הוּא

G. On this basis [it is ruled] that they unbind a vow on account of something that happened later on.

מִכַּאן שֶׁפּוֹתְחִין בְּנוֹלָד

H. And as to the rabbis [in opposition to Eliezer's rule]: what is their reason?

וְרַבָּנָן מַאי טַעֲמַיְיהוּ,

I. They argue: Did these men die?

קָסָבְרֵי הָנְהוּ מִי מָיְיתֵי

J. Now said R. Yohanan in the name of R. Simeon b. Yohai,

וְהָא אָמַר ר' יוֹחָנָן מִשּׁוּם ר' שִׁמְעוֹן בָּן יוֹחַי,

K. Wherever *nissim* [quarreling] or *nissavim* [standing] is mentioned, the reference is only to Dathan and Abiram (Ex. 2:13).

כָּל מָקוֹם שֶׁנֶּאֱמַר נִצִּים וְנִצָּבִים אֵינָן אֶלָּא דָּתָן וַאֲבִירָם.

L. But, said Resh Laqish,

אֶלָּא אָמַר ר"ל (רֵישׁ לָקִישׁ)

M. They lost their money.

שֶׁיָּרְדוּ מִנִּכְסֵיהָן.

Vocabulary

what is the reason	מ"ט (מַאי טַעְמָא)	they argue	קָסָבְרֵי
		they died	מְיִיתֵי
their reason	טַעֲמַיְיהוּ	their money	נִכְסֵיהָן

This is a complicated passage, and we shall have to work our way through it, step by step.

First, Eliezer's reasoning.

The Talmud here takes for granted that we know something that it says elsewhere—later on in this same passage, in fact. It says that Jethro was anxious about Moses's safety, since Moses was his son-in-law and friend. Therefore, Jethro made Moses take a vow that he would not go back to Egypt because there were men in Egypt who wanted to kill him.

Now in the light of that story, what do we have in Ex. 4:19?

God tells Moses in Midian to go back to Egypt. Why? Because the men who wanted to kill him are all dead.

But when Moses took the vow these same men were alive.

It seems that God has untied the vow of Moses because something that happened after the vow justified doing so.

And that is precisely Eliezer's claim: You may untie a vow on the basis of something that happens after the vow is taken.

Why? What is his "reason?" His reason is that God untied the vow of Moses on the basis of something that happened after Moses took the vow. Death is a new fact. A new fact serves as a good basis.

But the rabbis do not see things the way Eliezer does. They, too, read the same passage of Scripture. But they must read it in some other way since they do not concede that Eliezer is on firm ground.

How do they read Scripture's tale?

Very simply: they deny the men had died! Moses went back to Egypt because God ordered him to do so, not because God absolved his vow.

How do the rabbis prove that these men did not die?

They identify the men whom Moses was afraid would kill him. And then they maintain that these same men were not dead when Moses went back to Egypt.

How do they know?

Because the language used with reference to the men—Ex. 2:13—speaks of two Hebrews who "strove together." The verse is as follows:

> And when he went out on the second day, behold, two men of the Hebrews fought together (nissim).

Again, look at Ex. 5:20:

> And they met Moses and Aaron who had stood (nissavim) in the way.

And compare that verse with Num. 16:27:

> And Dathan and Abiram came out and stood.

The same people who stood in one place, stood in the other: Dathan and Abiram. And they were the ones who had had the fight that caused Moses to run away.

So they were not dead when Moses returned to Egypt—that is shown by Num. 16:27, which tells of Dathan and Abiram in the rebellion of Korah.

It follows that they were still alive, and Moses therefore did not return because of something that happened after he took his vow.

Essentially what sages do is to explain the proof of Eliezer in such a way that it will no longer prove his point.

This is a good mode of argument. But it leaves one small problem.

God would appear to tell Moses something that is not true.

Dathan and Abiram, we now have shown, were still alive.

And God has told Moses, "The men who wanted to kill you have died."

What could God have meant? This is the question that Resh Laqish answers.

Resh Laqish says: They did not die. But they had lost all their money. And someone who becomes poor is as good as dead.

We shall now go over the proof that a poor man is like a dead man. What we shall see is that the reference to the death of the men who wanted to kill Moses, Dathan and Abiram, really means they had lost their money.

This brings us to the end of this passage (E-J) and to Joshua b. Levi's statement about a group of people—four in all—who are as good as dead.

A. Said R. Joshua b. Levi,

אריב״ל (אָמַר רַבִּי יְהוֹשׁוּעַ בֶּן לֵוִי)

B. Any person who does not have children is deemed to be like a dead person,

כָּל אָדָם שָׁאֵין לוֹ בָּנִים חָשׁוּב כְּמֵת

C. since it is said, Give me children, or else I am dead (Gen. 30:1).

שֶׁנֶּאֱמַר הָבָה לִי בָנִים וְאִם אַיִן מֵתָה אָנֹכִי.

D. And it has been taught:

וְתַנְיָא

E. Four [types of people] are deemed to be like a dead person:

אַרְבָּעָה חֲשׁוּבִין כְּמֵת

F. a poor man, and a person who is a leper; and a blind man, and one who does not have children.

עָנִי וּמְצוֹרָע וְסוּמָא וּמִי שָׁאֵין לוֹ בָּנִים.

G. A poor man, as it is written, For all the men [who sought your life] are dead.

עָנִי דִּכְתִיב כִּי מֵתוּ כָּל הָאֲנָשִׁים.

H. A leper, as it is written, [And Aaron looked at Miriam, and behold, she was a leper. And Aaron said to

מְצוֹרָע דִּכְתִיב (וַיִּפֶן אַהֲרֹן אֶל מִרְיָם וְהִנֵּה מְצֹרָעַת

Moses,] Let her not be as one who is dead (Num. 12:10-12).

וַיֹּאמֶר אַהֲרֹן אֶל מֹשֶׁה)....אַל נָא תְהִי כַמֵּת

I. A blind person, as it is written, He has set me in dark places, as they that be dead of old (Lamentations 3:6).

וְסוּמָא דִּכְתִיב בְּמַחֲשַׁכִּים הוֹשִׁיבַנִי כְּמֵתֵי עוֹלָם

J. And one who has no children, as it is said, Give me children or else I am dead (Gen. 30:1).

וּמִי שֶׁאֵין לוֹ בָנִים דִּכְתִיב הָבָה לִי בָנִים וְאִם אַיִן מֵתָה אָנֹכִי.

Vocabulary

is deemed	חָשׁוּב	a leper	מְצוֹרָע
a poor man	עָנִי	a blind man	סוּמָא

The proposition is simple. These four sorts of people are as good as dead. The issue is, How shall we prove our point?

The answer is that Scripture is proof.

The childless person is like a corpse, just as is said in Gen. 30:1.

A poor man is like a dead man—on the basis of what God says about Dathan and Abiram.

A leper is like a corpse, as Aaron says.

A blind person is like a dead person, because Lamentations 3:6 is understood to mean, God has put me in dark places, just as the blind, who are accounted as long since dead.

Our passage draws to a close. Yet it leaves open a question that the Talmud now will want to answer carefully.

If God absolved Moses from his vow before Jethro and allowed him to return to Egypt, then what about Jethro? What did he make of all this?

Should God or Moses not have told Jethro what was going on?

Indeed, that is required.

That Talmud then says—without explaining why—if you take a vow in front of someone else, then you must be before that person to untie the vow.

This is the basis for understanding the next paragraphs of the Talmud: an important *halakhah,* then a relevant *aggadic* story. And in a moment we shall see that very consideration—untying a vow in the presence of the person who originally witnessed or heard it—led the person who put our Talmud together to go on to just this matter. He will tell us so explicitly.

12. Expanding the Explanation

Moses's vow not to go back to Egypt was absolved. But Jethro knew nothing about it. That hardly makes sense. Moses will go along, and Jethro will believe that Moses has violated his vow. Jethro will assume that Moses was disrespectful to God, and this is not the right way to act.

The Talmudic discussion, therefore, must turn to this question and explain under what circumstances a vow is to be untied. If you looked at the Mishnah-passage, you surely would not have predicted that the discussion would move in this direction.

Yet because of what we have just said, we now realize that it is absolutely necessary to raise just this topic, at just this time. We will raise the general question first—untying a vow in the very presence of the person who witnessed it to begin with—and then link our observation to the discussion we have just concluded, about Moses in Midian.

A further important trait of what follows is that we move from a *halakhic* to an *aggadic* passage. First, we treat what one should or should not do. We engage in an important discussion of rules and laws, of how things are done and the way things should be done—*halakhah*.

Yet, without warning, we turn to an *aggadic* tale about Nebuchadnezzar, the king of the Babylonians who destroyed the first Temple and Jerusalem in 586 B.C.E., and Zedekiah, the King of the Jews, who was conquered and taken away into exile. For a brief moment, you might imagine that this *aggadic* tale is simply thrown in without any purpose. But, of course, the Talmud is a carefully organized discussion, and you should be able to explain without difficulty why the story is introduced.

The story tells us why we should keep the law we have just discussed. It takes the law and spells out its importance.

Let us first read the concluding unit of our complete passage of the Talmud and then return to these two questions.

IV. A. It was taught:

תַּנְיָא

B. a person who took a vow [against] benefiting from his fellow

הַמּוּדָר הֲנָאָה מֵחֲבֵירוֹ

C. they unbind him [from his vow] only in his [the neighbor's] presence.

אֵין מַתִּירִין לוֹ אֶלָּא בְּפָנָיו

D. What is the source of this teaching?

מנה"מ (מְנָא הָא מִלְתָא)

E. Said R. Nahman,

אָמַר ר׳ נַחְמָן

F. Since it is written, And the Lord said to Moses in Midian, Go, return into Egypt, for all the men who sought your life are dead.

דִּכְתִיב וַיֹּאמֶר ה׳ אֶל מֹשֶׁה בְּמִדְיָן לֵךְ שׁוּב מִצְרַיִם כִּי מֵתוּ כָּל הָאֲנָשִׁים

G. He said to him, In Midian you took a vow.

אָמַר לוֹ בְּמִדְיָן נָדַרְתָּ

H. Go and have your vow unbound in Midian.

לֵךְ וְהַתֵּר נִדְרְךָ בְּמִדְיָן

I. [How do we know that Moses vowed in Midian?]

J. Since it is said, And Moses was content [to dwell with the man] (Ex. 2:21).

דִּכְתִיב וַיּוֹאֶל מֹשֶׁה (לָשֶׁבֶת אֶת הָאִישׁ)

K. Now alah means only 'an oath'

אֵין אָלָה אֶלָּא שְׁבוּעָה

L. since it is written, And he has taken an (alah) oath of him (Ezek. 17:13).

דִּכְתִיב וַיָּבֵא אֹתוֹ בְּאָלָה.

Vocabulary

a person who took a vow   הַמּוּדָר

benefit	הֲנָאָה
What is the source of this teaching?	מנה״מ (מְנָא הָא מִלְתָא)
go	לַד
have unbound	הַתֵּר
oath	אָלָה

V. A. And also against King Nebuchadnezzar he rebelled, who had made him take an oath by God (II Chron. 36:13).

וְגַם בַּמֶּלֶךְ נְבוּכַדְנֶצַּר מָרָד אֲשֶׁר הִשְׁבִּיעוֹ בֵּאלֹהִים (חיים)

B. What was the character of his rebellion?

מַאי מְרְדּוּתֵיהּ?

C. Zedekiah found [Nebuchadnezzar],

אַשְׁכְּחֵיהּ צִדְקִיָּה

D. that he was eating a live rabbit.

דַּהֲוָה קָאָכִיל אַרְנְבָא חַיָה.

E. He [Nebuchadnezzar] said to him, Take an oath to me that you will not tell on me,

א״ל (אָמַר לֵיהּ) אִישְׁתְּבַע לִי דְּלָא מְגַלִּיתָ עִילָוַי

F. and that a word [on this] will not get out.

וְלָא תִיפּוֹק מִילְתָא.

G. He took an oath.

אִישְׁתְּבַע;

H. Later on Zedekiah was pained.

לְסוֹף הֲוָה קָא מִצְטַעַר צִדְקִיָּהוּ בְּנַפְשֵׁיהּ

I. He made inquiry for his vow [and had it unbound],

אִיתְּשִׁיל אַשְׁבוּעָתֵיהּ

J. and he said [what he had seen Nebuchadnezzar eating].

וַאֲמַר.

K. Nebuchadnezzar heard that

שָׁמַע נְבוּכַדְנֶצַּר

64

they were making fun of him.

L. He sent and summoned the Sanhedrin and Zedekiah.

הְקָא מְבַזִּין לֵיהּ.

שְׁלַח וְאַיְיתִי סַנְהֶדְרִין וְצִדְקִיָּהוּ.

M. He said to them, Have you seen what Zedekiah did?

אָמַר לְהוֹן חֲזֵיתוּן מַאי קָא עָבֵיד צִדְקִיָּהוּ,

N. Did he not take an oath by the name of Heaven that he would not tell on me?

לָאו הָכִי אִשְׁתְּבַע בִּשְׁמָא דִּשְׁמַיָּא דְּלָא מְנַלִּינָא,

O. They said to him, He was absolved of his oath.

א"ל (אָמְרוּ לֵיהּ) אִיתְּשְׁלִי אַשְׁבוּעָתָא.

P. He said to them, Are people absolved of oaths?

א"ל מִתְשְׁלִין אַשְׁבוּעָתָא,

Q. They said to him, Yes.

אָמְרֵי לֵיהּ אִין.

R. He said to them, "In his presence, or even not in his presence?"

אָמַר לְהוֹ בְּפָנָיו אוֹ אֲפִילוּ שֶׁלֹּא בְּפָנָיו.

S. They said to him, [Only] in his presence.

אָמְרֵי לֵיהּ בְּפָנָיו.

T. He said to them, "And you people—what have you done?

אָמַר לְהוֹן וְאַתּוּן מַאי עֲבָדִיתוּן,

U. Why did you not say so to Zedekiah?

מַאי טַעְמָא לָא אֲמָרִיתוּן לְצִדְקִיָּהוּ.

V. Forthwith, The elders of the daughter of Zion sit upon the ground and keep silence (Lamentations 2:10).

מִיַּד יֵשְׁבוּ לָאָרֶץ יִדְּמוּ זִקְנֵי בַת צִיּוֹן.

W. Said R. Isaac,

אָמַר רַבִּי יִצְחָק

X. That they removed the pillows from under them.

שֶׁשָּׁמְטוּ כָּרִים מִתַּחְתֵּיהֶם.

Vocabulary

his rebellion	מְרַדוּתֵיהּ	by the name of Heaven	בִּשְׁמָא דִשְׁמַיָא
found him	אַשְׁכְּחֵיהּ		
eating	קָאָכִיל	tell	מַנְלִינָא
a live rabbit	אַרְנְבָא חָיָה	was absolved	אִיתְשְׁלִי
tell on him	מְנַלִיתָ עִילָוֵי	yes	אִין
get out	תִּיפּוֹק	in his presence	בְּפָנָיו
a word	מִילְתָא	to them	לְהוֹן
he took an oath	אִישְׁתְּבַע	and you	וְאַתּוּן
made inquiry	אִיתְשִׁיל	what have you done	מַאי עֲבַדִיתוּן
for his vow	אַשְׁבוּעָתֵיהּ		
make fun of	מְבַזִּין	you said	אַמְרִיתוּן
summoned	אַיְיתִי	removed	שְׁמְטוּ
have you seen?	חֲזַיתוּן	pillows	כָּרִים
took an oath	אִישְׁתְּבַע		

et us first analyze the story (V.A-X), and then try to find its relevance to the larger discussion that it concludes.

The story begins with the citation of a verse of Scripture. If we understand the verse properly, we will know why the story-teller made up the story.

The verse has two significant elements: (1) the rebellion of Zedekiah (not named, but look up the verse and you will see him), and (2) the matter of the oath.

Nebuchadnezzar imposed the oath. The cited verse makes that clear, "who had made him take an oath." What was the cause of the oath? The fact that Nebuchadnezzar was doing something he did not want anyone to know about. The worst thing the story-teller can imagine is eating a live rabbit. A rabbit is not *kosher* food for Jews. Moreover, the story-teller is disgusted by the idea of eating any live animal. So the Babylonian king Nebuchadnezzar made Zedekiah take an oath not to tell anyone that the king ate a live rabbit.

The first part of the story ends with the oath (G). The narrator then adds that Zedekiah regretted his oath, had himself absolved from it, and reported what he had seen.

Nebuchadnezzar was rightly angry. He thought Zedekiah had violated his oath (K-N). He did not know that the sages had released the oath (Q). Then Nebuchadnezzar shows the wisdom of the law. One may untie an oath only in the presence of the person who witnessed the oath to begin with. The sages had made a gross error. It was, moreover, an injustice. So, the story ends, the sages (V) had to keep quiet. They had no answer to the Babylonian king. W-X add that the sages were unworthy and were deposed.

The story underlines the value and wisdom of the law. A sage must deal with a vow in the presence of the person who is affected by the vow, not only in the presence of the person who took the vow.

Now let us ask ourselves, if we want to make a general rule about the relationship between *halakhah* and *aggadah,* what would be the rule?

Does *aggadah*—as we see it here—simply tell a nice story? Is it thrown in merely to entertain us? Or does the *aggadah* make a point? And is it an important point?

I think the answer is self-evident. The *aggadah* is more than an amusing story. It is a serious tale and makes an important point. The point is precisely the same as the purpose of the *halakhah.* And both are important, equally and reciprocally.

Aggadah and *halakhah,* when properly brought together and made into neighbors, talk to one another. Both say the same thing. But one says its truth as an abstract rule—a statement of how things are done in general. The other says its truth in a concrete way. *Aggadah* tells a tale about specific people at one point and in one place. To be sure, the people are not ordinary. They are important folk—men and women worth remembering and imitating.

As you learn other passages of the Talmud, you will want to discover the relationship between a law and a story, between *halakhah* and *aggadah.* The Talmud's arrangers and writers present the two together, and it should be possible to make some sense of the two as they march down the page in single file.

Now let us turn back to the *halakhic* discussion [IV A-L], which is easier. We notice that the passage begins with a general rule (A-C). If a person takes a vow not to make use of anything belonging to someone else, the vow can be untied only in the presence of that other person. We know why this rule has to be introduced at this point. Moses left Midian, we remember, in what would seem to be a violation of the vow he took for Jethro. And the Talmud immediately reminds us of just that fact.

The Talmud asks (D), "How do we know that this rule is so?"

We, of course, know the answer—Scripture is the source of all rules.

So (E) Nahman cites a verse (Ex. 4:19). Notice that Nahman reads the verse in an odd way. We should expect, "And the Lord said to Moses in Midian, 'Go, return to Egypt.' " But Nahman reads, "And the Lord said to Moses, 'In Midian go—then return to Egypt.' " His sense of the verse is, "Go back to Midian." And why? "To have your vow annulled. For you took your vow in Midian and, therefore, you have to untie the vow in the presence of the people before whom you took it."

In order to make sense of the passage, we have to supply the question (I): How do we know that there was a vow?

At the outset of our discussion, we introduced the fact that Moses had taken a vow to Jethro. The Talmudic discussion took this fact for granted but did not spell it out. Remember that we explained Eliezer's ruling, "A new fact will serve as a pretext for untying a vow," in terms of God's releasing Moses from the vow he had taken in Midian. But at that point we had no knowledge of such a vow.

Here is the proof, then, that there was such a vow, and, further, this same proof is just as relevant at the earlier passage—Hisda's contribution—as it is now.

The proof is based on a play on words.

Scripture says, *And Moses was content (va-yo'el) to dwell with the man* (Ex. 2:21).

The word *va-yo'el* comes from the root *alah*, which means to take an oath.

This is proved by the use of the word in Ezek. 17:13, *And has taken an oath (alah)*.

So Ex. 2:21 is to be read, *And Moses took an oath to dwell with the man*

(Jethro).

Is this far-fetched?

The answer is not obvious. On the one hand, the context of Ex. 2:21 surely demands that we read, "*And Moses was content to dwell with the man.*" Yet the word *content* has another meaning—take an oath. And we are able to show that this other meaning is sensible. So it is at least possible to read the verse the way our passage wants us to read it.

You must notice one thing: the process of explaining the verse to prove that Moses took an oath to Jethro is a process of discovery. That is, the person who made up this proof wants to find the meaning of a word. He discovers what it means in one passage and introduces that meaning to the passage he is trying to interpret.

Is this what we do in a biology lab or in math? Is this a fair duplication of the processes of discovery that we use in our studies of modern science or history?

The methods have similarities and differences.

How do we know that Moses vowed in Midian? The question tells the story.

We start out to prove a specific proposition. We, therefore, look for a use of the word in question that conforms to what we want the word to mean.

Our purpose is not to test or to discover knowledge. It is, rather, to confirm and prove what we already think.

So this is not a process of discovery entirely like what you may have observed in science or in history. It is a different and distinct way of thinking.

That does not mean you should reject it. Rather, you have to understand the world of the Talmud, the way in which the Talmud's authorities *think,* in a different way. Indeed, one of the things worth learning from a book such as the Talmud is a completely different way of thinking from our own.

13. The Talmud All Together

BABYLONIAN TALMUD NEDARIM 64A-65A

Once more we want to see the entire passage of the Talmud as a single unit. But now our purpose is more precise. Not only do we want to see all the elements together—as we did in Chapter 8—we also want to explain the purpose of the person who put the present passage together. For we are looking for the first time at a complete discussion of the Talmud, beginning with the citation of a given passage of the Mishnah and ending with the conclusion of that discussion. What follows in the Talmud is the citation of another passage of the Mishnah. So here it is not only all together, but it is also complete. We, therefore, have a better opportunity than we did before to make sense of the Talmud as a whole.

First we read the passage from beginning to end, with the English translation. Notice the points at which the Talmud is in Aramaic, and those at which it expresses its ideas in Hebrew. See whether you can tell when Hebrew will be used and when you are going to find Aramaic. Does it make sense to offer this theory: When the Talmud wants to cite the Mishnah or to give teachings that belong in the Mishnah, it uses the language of the Mishnah, which is Hebrew. When the Talmud speaks in the voice of its own authorities—the rabbis of its own day—it speaks in Aramaic, which is the language they used. Test this theory here, and try it out in the other units as well. You will see some interesting things.

Now let us proceed to read the complete passage but with the sentences divided and with the English words provided alongside. The next time you do this, it will be without my help.

1	Rabbi Eliezer says:	רַבִּי אֱלִיעֶזֶר אוֹמֵר:
	They untie [a vow] for a person on account of the honor of his father and his mother.	פּוֹתְחִין לְאָדָם בִּכְבוֹד אָבִיו וְאִמּוֹ;

70

And sages prohibit [keep it
tied].

וַחֲכָמִים אוֹסְרִין.

2   Said Rabbi Sadoq:

אָמַר רַבִּי צָדוֹק:

Before they untie [a vow] for a
person on account of father
or mother, let them untie it
for that person on account of
the honor of the
Omnipresent.

עַד שֶׁפּוֹתְחִין לוֹ
בִּכְבוֹד אָבִיו וְאִמּוֹ,
יִפְתְּחוּ לוֹ בִּכְבוֹד הַמָּקוֹם,

[And] if so, there will be no
vows [at all]!

אִם כֵּן אֵין נְדָרִים!

3   And sages agree with Rabbi
Eliezer concerning a matter
[about which one vowed]
between father and mother,
that they untie it for the
person on account of the
honor of father and mother.

וּמוֹדִים חֲכָמִים לְרַבִּי אֱלִיעֶזֶר
בְּדָבָר שֶׁבֵּינוֹ לְבֵין אָבִיו וְאִמּוֹ,
שֶׁפּוֹתְחִין לוֹ בִּכְבוֹד אָבִיו וְאִמּוֹ.

4   And furthermore did Rabbi
Eliezer say:

וְעוֹד אָמַר רַבִּי אֱלִיעֶזֶר:

They untie [a vow] on
account of something that
happened [later on]

פּוֹתְחִין בַּנּוֹלָד;

And sages prohibit

וַחֲכָמִים אוֹסְרִין.

5   How so?

כֵּיצַד?

[If] he said, Qonam—that I
shall not derive benefit from
so-and-so

אָמַר: קוֹנָם שֶׁאֵינִי
נֶהֱנֶה לְאִישׁ פְּלוֹנִי,

and he [so-and-so] became a
scribe

וְנַעֲשָׂה סוֹפֵר,

or was going to marry off his
son very soon

אוֹ שֶׁהָיָה מַשִּׂיא אֶת בְּנוֹ בְּקָרוֹב,

6 and he said, If I had known
that he would become a
scribe

וְאָמַר: אִלּוּ הָיִיתִי יוֹדֵעַ
שֶׁהוּא נַעֲשָׂה סוֹפֵר,

or that he would marry off his
son very soon
I should not have taken a vow

אוֹ שֶׁהוּא מַשִּׂיא אֶת בְּנוֹ בְּקָרוֹב-

לֹא הָיִיתִי נוֹדֵר.

7 Qonam against this house,
that I shall not enter it and it
was made into a synagogue

קוֹנָם לְבַיִת זֶה שֶׁאֵינִי נִכְנָם,
וְנַעֲשָׂה בֵית הַכְּנֶסֶת,

[if] he said, If I had known
that it would be made into a
synagogue, I should not have
taken a vow

אָמַר: אִלּוּ הָיִיתִי יוֹדֵעַ
שֶׁהוּא נַעֲשָׂה בֵית הַכְּנֶסֶת,
לֹא הָיִיתִי נוֹדֵר-

8 Rabbi Eliezer unties [the vow]

רַבִּי אֱלִיעֶזֶר מַתִּיר;

And sages prohibit [keep it
tied].

וַחֲכָמִים אוֹסְרִין.

I. A. What is [the meaning of]
"There will be no vows?

מַאי אֵין נְדָרִים?

B. Said Abbaye,

אָמַר אַבַּיֵי

C. If so, no vows may be
unbound.

אִם כֵּן אֵין נְדָרִים נִיתָּרִין יָפָה.

D. And Raba said,

וְרָבָא אָמַר

E. If so, Vows will not be
brought for inquiry [and
absolution] to a sage.

א״כ (אִם כֵּן) אֵין נְדָרִים
נִשְׁאָלִין
לְחָכָם.

F. We have learned:

תְּנַן

G. And sages concede to R.

וּמוֹדִין חֲכָמִים לְרַבִּי אֱלִיעֶזֶר

Eliezer that in a matter involving himself and his father and mother, they do release him by reason of the honor of his father and his mother.

כִּדְבָר שֶׁכֵּינוּ לְכֵין אָבִיו וְאִמּוֹ שֶׁפּוֹתְחִים לוֹ בִּכְבוֹד אָבִיו וְאִמּוֹ.

H. Certainly, this accords with Abbaye, who said, If so, no vows may be unbound;

כִּשְׁלָמָא לְאַבַּיֵי דְּאָמַר אִם כֵּן אֵין נְדָרִים נִיתָּרִין

I. here, if he has been so impudent, he is impudent.

הָכָא כֵּיוָן דְּאִיחְצֵף לֵיהּ הָא אִיחְצֵף לֵיהּ.

J. But so far as Raba is concerned, who said, If so, vows will not be brought for inquiry [and absolution] to a sage,

אֶלָּא לְרָבָא דְּאָמַר אִם כֵּן אֵין נְדָרִים נִשְׁאָלִין לְחָכָם

K. in this case, why do they unbind [the vow]?

הָכָא אַמַּאי פּוֹתְחִין,

L. I shall tell you;

אַמְרֵי

M. since all vows cannot be [declared not binding] without a sage,

כֵּיוָן דְּכָל נִדְרֵי לָא סַנְיָא לְהוֹן דְּלָאו חָכָם

N. here too they [sages] will declare the vow unbound

הָכָא נַמִּי פּוֹתְחִין.

II. A. R. Eliezer says, They unbind a vow on account of something that happened later on.

רַבִּי אֱלִיעֶזֶר פּוֹתְחִין בְּנוֹלָד כוּ׳

B. What is the reason of R. Eliezer?

מ״ט דְּרַבִּי אֱלִיעֶזֶר,

C. Said R. Hisda,

אָמַר רַב חִסְדָּא,

D. Since Scripture has said,

דְּאָמַר קְרָא:

E. [And the Lord said to Moses in Midian, Go, return to Egypt,] for all the men [who sought to kill you] are dead (Ex. 4:19).

כִּי מֵתוּ כָּל הָאֲנָשִׁים,

F. Now death was something that happened later on.

וְהָא מִיתָה דְּנוֹלָד הוּא

G. On this basis [it is ruled] that they unbind a vow on account of something that happened later on.

מִכָּאן שֶׁפּוֹתְחִין בְּנוֹלָד

H. And as to the rabbis [in opposition to Eliezer's rule]: what is their reason?

וְרַבָּנָן מַאי טַעֲמָיְיהוּ,

I. They argue: Did these men die?

קָסָבְרֵי הֶנְהוּ מִי מָיְיתֵי

J. Now said R. Yohanan in the name of R. Simeon b. Yohai,

וְהָא אָמַר ר׳ יוֹחָנָן מִשּׁוּם ר׳ שִׁמְעוֹן בֶּן יוֹחַי,

K. Wherever nissim [quarreling] or nissavim [standing] is mentioned, the reference is only to Dathan and Abiram (Ex. 2:13).

כָּל מָקוֹם שֶׁנֶּאֱמַר נִצִּים וְנִצָּבִים אֵינָן אֶלָּא דָּתָן וַאֲבִירָם.

L. But, said Resh Laqish,

אֶלָּא אָמַר ר״ל (רֵישׁ לָקִישׁ)

M. They lost their money.

שֶׁיָּרְדוּ מִנִּכְסֵיהֶן.

III. A. Said R. Joshua b. Levi,

אריב״ל (אָמַר רַבִּי יְהוֹשֻׁעַ בֶּן לֵוִי)

B. Any person who does not have children is deemed to be like a dead person,

כָּל אָדָם שֶׁאֵין לוֹ בָּנִים חָשׁוּב כָּמֵת

C. since it is said, Give me children, or else I am dead (Gen. 30:1).

שֶׁנֶּאֱמַר הָבָה לִי בָנִים וְאִם אַיִן מֵתָה אָנֹכִי.

D. And it has been taught:

וְתַנְיָא

E. Four [types of people] are deemed to be like a dead person:

אַרְבָּעָה חֲשׁוּבִין כְּמֵת

F. a poor man, and a person who is a leper, and a blind man, and one who does not have children.

עָנִי וּמְצוֹרָע
וְסוּמָא
וּמִי שֶׁאֵין לוֹ בָּנִים.

G. A poor man, as it is written, For all the men [who sought your life] are dead.

עָנִי דִּכְתִיב
כִּי מֵתוּ כָּל הָאֲנָשִׁים.

H. A leper, as it is written, [And Aaron looked at Miriam, and behold, she was a leper. And Aaron said to Moses,] Let her not be as one who is dead (Num. 12:10-12).

מְצוֹרָע דִּכְתִיב
(וַיִּפֶן אַהֲרֹן אֶל מִרְיָם
וְהִנֵּה מְצֹרָעַת
וַיֹּאמֶר אַהֲרֹן אֶל מֹשֶׁה)....אַל נָא
תְהִי כַּמֵּת

I. A blind person, as it is written, He has set me in dark places, as they that be dead of old (Lamentations 3:6).

וְסוּמָא דִּכְתִיב
בְּמַחֲשַׁכִּים הוֹשִׁיבַנִי
כְּמֵתֵי עוֹלָם

J. And one who has no children, as it is said, Give me children or else I am dead (Gen. 30:1).

וּמִי שֶׁאֵין לוֹ בָּנִים דִּכְתִיב הָבָה
לִי בָנִים וְאִם אַיִן מֵתָה אָנֹכִי.

IV. A. It was taught:

תַּנְיָא

B. a person who took a vow [against] benefiting from his fellow

הַמֻּדָּר הֲנָאָה
מֵחֲבֵירוֹ

C. they unbind him [from his vow] only in his [the neighbor's] presence.

אֵין מַתִּירִין לוֹ
אֶלָּא בְּפָנָיו.

75

D. What is the source of this teaching?

מְנָה"מ (מְנָא הָא מִלְּתָא)

E. Said R. Nahman,

אָמַר ר׳ נַחְמָן

F. Since it is written, And the Lord said to Moses in Midian, Go, return into Egypt, for all the men who sought your life are dead.

דִּכְתִיב וַיֹּאמֶר ה׳
אֶל מֹשֶׁה בְּמִדְיָן לֵךְ שׁוּב מִצְרַיִם
כִּי מֵתוּ כָּל הָאֲנָשִׁים

G. He said to him, "In Midian you took a vow.

אָמַר לוֹ בְּמִדְיָן
נָדַרְתָּ

H. Go and have your vow unbound in Midian.

לֵךְ וְהַתֵּר נִדְרְךָ בְּמִדְיָן

I. [How do we know that Moses vowed in Midian?]

J. Since it is said, And Moses was content [to dwell with the man] (Ex. 2:21).

דִּכְתִיב וַיּוֹאֶל מֹשֶׁה
(לָשֶׁבֶת אֶת הָאִישׁ)

K. Now *alah* means only 'an oath',

אֵין אָלָה אֶלָּא שְׁבוּעָה

L. since it is written, And he has taken an (*alah*) oath of him (Ezek. 17:13).

דִּכְתִיב וַיָּבֵא אֹתוֹ בְּאָלָה.

V. A. And also against King Nebuchadnezzar he rebelled, who had made him take an oath by God (II Chron. 36:13).

וְגַם בַּמֶּלֶךְ נְבוּכַדְנֶצַּר
מָרָד אֲשֶׁר הִשְׁבִּיעוֹ
בֵּאלֹהִים (חיים)

B. What was the character of his rebellion?

מַאי מְרִדּוּתֵיהּ?

C. Zedekiah found [Nebuchadnezzar],

אַשְׁכְּחֵיהּ צִדְקִיָּה

D. that he was eating a live rabbit.

דַּהֲוָה קָאֲכִיל אַרְנְבָא חַיָּה.

76

E. He [Nebuchadnezzar] said to him, Take an oath to me that you will not tell on me,

F. and that a word [on this] will not get out.

G. He took an oath.

H. Later on Zedekiah was pained.

I. He made inquiry for his vow [and had it unbound],

J. and he said [what he had seen Nebuchadnezzar eating].

K. Nebuchadnezzar heard that they were making fun of him.

L. He sent and summoned the Sanhedrin and Zedekiah.

M. He said to them, Have you seen what Zedekiah did?

N. Did he not take an oath by the name of Heaven that he would not tell on me?

O. They said to him, He was absolved of his oath.

P. He said to them, Are people absolved of oaths?

Q. They said to him, Yes.

R. He said to them, "In his presence, or even not in his presence?"

S. They said to him, [Only] in his presence.

א״ל (אֲמַר לֵיהּ)

אִשְׁתְּבַע לִי דְּלָא מְגַלֵּית עִילָוַי

וְלָא תִיפּוֹק מִילְּתָא.

אִשְׁתְּבַע;

לְסוֹף הֲוָה קָא מִצְטַעֵר צִדְקִיָּהוּ בְּנַפְשֵׁיהּ

אִיתְּשִׁיל אַשְׁבוּעָתֵיהּ

וַאֲמַר.

שְׁמַע נְבוּכַדְנֶצַּר דְּקָא מְבַזּוּן לֵיהּ.

שְׁלַח וְאַיְיתִי סַנְהֶדְרִין וְצִדְקִיָּהוּ.

אֲמַר לְהוֹן חֲזִיתוּן מַאי קָא עָבֵיד צִדְקִיָּהוּ,

לָאו הָכִי אִשְׁתְּבַע בִּשְׁמָא דִּשְׁמַיָּא דְּלָא מְגַלֵּינָא,

א״ל (אֲמַרוּ לֵיהּ) אִיתְּשִׁלי אַשְׁבוּעָתָא.

א״ל מִתְשְׁלִין אַשְׁבוּעָתָא,

אָמְרִי לֵיהּ אִין.

אֲמַר לְהוּ בְּפָנָיו אוֹ אֲפִילוּ שֶׁלֹּא בְּפָנָיו.

אָמְרִי לֵיהּ בְּפָנָיו.

T. He said to them, "And you people—what have you done?

אָמַר לְהוֹן וְאַתּוּן מַאי עֲבָדִיתוּן,

U. Why did you not say so to Zedekiah?

מַאי טַעְמָא לָא אֲמָרִיתוּן לְצִדְקַיָּהוּ.

V. Forthwith, The elders of the daughter of Zion sit upon the ground and keep silence [Lamentations 2:10].

מִיַּד יַשְׁבוּ לָאָרֶץ יִדְּמוּ זִקְנֵי בַת צִיּוֹן.

W. Said R. Isaac,

אָמַר רַבִּי יִצְחָק

X. That they removed the pillows from under them.

שֶׁשָּׁמְטוּ כָּרִים מִתַּחְתֵּיהֶם.

Now that you have seen the passage as a whole, you should be able to understand why I divided it to present to you. Go back over these divisions and decide whether or not you agree with my guess as to what they should be.

A second exercise will not surprise you: Can you explain why the person arranged the passage of the Talmud this way? To answer the question, try to make an outline of the passage. See where the chief headings lie. It may help you to use my chapter-divisions.

Now with such an outline in hand, I want you to consider a statement many people make about the Talmud.

They say it is disorganized.

Many people who know the Talmud in some measure and have studied it for a while claim that the Talmud is not put together coherently. You just go from this to that, then to another. Perhaps that is so, perhaps not.

On the basis of this sample, what do you think? Do you see the Talmud as disorganized and merely a jumble of materials? Or does it appear to be carefully constructed? You should be able to back up your opinion with arguments based upon your outline.

Can you explain to someone precisely why the person who put things together has done things this way—and not in some other?

What are the choices the editor had? What are the different ways that the material might have been presented? Can you discern why the editor decided to do things this particular way? Or is there no apparent reason?

I ask you these questions here because you have a whole passage of the Talmud before you: the Mishnah together with everything the Talmud chooses to tell us about that Mishnah. If you cannot make sense of the way in which the person who made up this passage has done the work, then you should conclude two things:

1. The Talmud is just a collection of things but not put together as a work worth your attention.

2. The Talmud is an anthology, not a piece of writing on which someone has spent time and hard thought.

But *if* you can isolate the materials that the person who made up our passage had in hand, and *if* you can then explain why that person put things together the way it was done, then what do you know?

You know the secret of the Talmud: what is Talmudic about the Talmud.

Let us explore that big *if*.

1. What are the basic elements, the sayings and stories, the citations and explanations, that make up our passage?

2. If you copy each one of these down on a card and lay it out on a table, which one would you choose first to begin a Talmud that you make up?

I am inclined to think that, after the Mishnah, the first thing you must do is explain what the Mishnah says. You have to answer the obvious and pressing questions that the Mishnah leaves open.

Then what must follow? Once you explain the Mishnah, you will have to explain—and expand—your explanation. And once you have done that, have you not used all your cards?

As I said at the outset of this little exercise, "What are the choices? What are the possibilities? And how has the person who arranged our Talmud ('made it up') decided things?"

When you have completed the next exercise in reviewing the Talmud as a whole, I shall have a different set of questions for you.

But first, reread the entire text— Mishnah, then Talmud— as it appears in the Talmud today. You should now be able to supply the commas and the periods, the paragraph divisions, and all the other things the Talmud— as it is printed—does not supply to make good sense of the whole.

רבי אליעזר אומר פותחין לאדם בכבוד אביו ואמו וחכמים
אוסרין אמר רבי צדוק עד שפותחין לו בכבוד אביו ואמו
יפתחו לו בכבוד המקום אם כן אין נדרים מודים חכמים לר'
אליעזר בדבר שבינו לבין אביו ואמו שפותחין לו בכבוד אביו ואמו
ועוד אמר רבי אליעזר פותחין בנולד וחכמים אוסרין כיצד אמר
קונם שאיני נהנה לאיש פלוני ונעשה סופר או שהיה משיא את
בנו ואמר אילו הייתי יודע שהוא נעשה סופר או שהיה משיא את
בנו בקרוב לא הייתי נודר קונם לבית זה שאיני נכנס ונעשה בית
הכנסת אמר אילו הייתי יודע שהוא נעשה בית הכנסת לא הייתי
נודר רבי אליעזר מתיר וחכמים אוסרין : גמ' מאי אין נדרים
אמר אביי אם כן אין נדרים ניתרין יפה ורבא אמר א״כ אין נדרים
נשאלין לחכם תנן ומודין חכמים לרבי אליעזר בדבר שבינו לבין
אביו ואמו שפותחים לו בכבוד אביו ואמו בשלמא לאביי דאמר אם
כן אין נדרים ניתרין הכא כיון דאיחצף ליה הא איחצף ליה אלא
לרבא דאמר אם כן אין נדרים נשאלין לחכם הכא אמאי פותחין
אמרי כיון דכל נדרי לא סגיא להון דלאו חכם הכא נמי פותחין :
ועוד אמר רבי אליעזר פותחין בנולד כו' : מ״ט דרבי אליעזר אמר
רב חסדא דאמר קרא כי מתו כל האנשים והא מיתה דנולד הוא
מכאן שפותחין בנולד ורבנן מאי טעמייהו קסברי הנהו מי מייתי
והא אמר ר'יוחנן משום ר'שמעון בן יוחי כל מקום שנאמר נצים
ונצבים אינן אלא דתן ואבירם אלא אמר ר״ל שירדו מנכסיהן
אריב״ל כל אדם שאין לו בנים חשוב כמת שנאמר הבה לי בנים
ואם אין מתה אנכי ותניא ארבעה חשובין כמת עני ומצורע וסומא
ומי שאין לו בנים עני דכתיב כי מתו כל האנשים מצורע דכתיב אל

80

נא תהי כמת וסומא דכתיב במחשכים הושיבני כמתי עולם ומי
שאין לו בנים דכתיב הבה לי בנים ואם מתה אין אנכי תניא
המודר הנאה מחבירו אין מתירין לו אלא בפניו מנה"מ אמר רב
נחמן דכתיב ויאמר ה' אל משה במדין לך שוב מצרים כי מתו כל
האנשים אמר לו במדין נדרת לך והתר נדרך במדין דכתיב ויואל
משה אין אלה אלא שבועה דכתיב ויבא אתו באלה וגם במלך
נבוכדנצר מרד אשר השביעו באלהים (חיים) מאי מרדותיה
אשכחיה צדקיה לנבוכדנצר דהוה קאכיל ארנבא חיה א"ל
אישתבע לי דלא מגלית עילוי ולא תיפוק מילתא אישתבע לסוף
הוה קא מצטער צדקיהו בנופיה איתשיל אשבועתיה ואמר שמע
נבוכדנצר דקא מבזין ליה שלח ואייתי סנהדרין וצדקיהו אמר להין
חזיתון מאי קא עביד צדקיהו לאו הכי אישתבע בשמא דשמיא דלא
מגלינא א"ל איתשיל אשבועתא]א"ל מתשלין אשבועתאן[אמרי
ליה אין אמר להו בפניו או אפילו שלא בפניו אמרי ליה בפניו
אמר להון ואתון מאי עבדיתון מאי טעמא לא אמריתון לצדקיהו
מיד ישבו לארץ ידמו זקני בת ציון אמר רבי יצחק ששמטו כרים
מתחתיהם.

ow you see the passage as a whole. You see it element by element, then with the parts linked together, and, finally, complete without interruption.

It is time to ask a different question.

Do you think the Talmud has done a good job explaining the Mishnah-passage?

What do you consider a "good job" to be? Specifically, go back to the Mishnah-passage itself, and see whether you can discern topics or problems that the person who put the Talmud together has ignored or chosen not to explore.

One question that is not answered is, Who says you may untie vows at all?

Another question is, What are other suitable grounds for the untying of a vow?

A third question is, What is the meaning of "a new fact?"

A fourth question is, Why do I need three examples of new facts? Why should Eliezer's position be spelled out at such length?

A fifth question is, What do we mean by a scribe? What is the meaning of the word *Qonam,* and how shall we define other words used in this passage?

These questions are not like one another. Some of them are trivial, others are basic. Some of them would add mere details. But if we dealt with others of them, we should have produced a different Talmudic passage from the one that we have studied.

The main thing to remember in this exercise is this: You must always use your own imagination. You must figure out the things a person might have done, so you can understand the things he or she actually has done.

What are the possibilities? What are the choices among which the person actually has made a selection? Only then shall we understand the purpose and the achievement that are before us. *Only when we realize what might have been will we truly understand what is.*

WHAT IS THE TALMUD?

This discussion of the choices someone has made allows us to ask our basic question in a new way.

For the Talmud is not simply "given"—that is, the way things *had* to be.

It represents a series of careful and deliberate choices, among many possibilities, of how someone wanted things to be.

That is to say, once we deal with Mishnah, we have certain jobs to do with Mishnah. These are done in a particular way—and not in some other—in the Talmud before us.

So when we ask, "What is the Talmud," we have a second basic question: What is the Talmud's conception of *how* the Mishnah should be explained and understood?

If we say, "In part, the Talmud is an explanation of the Mishnah," we have not said a lot. For we also have to say what we mean by "explanation of the Mishnah." I think you now can do this on the basis of the two Talmudic passages you have learned.

You will notice that the Talmud begins its work on Mishnah by attention to the Mishnah itself. That means the Talmud regards explanation as something that must be precise, direct, and relevant to the Mishnah. It begins not with examples or generalizations, not with stories, expansions of the law of Mishnah, or sermons about keeping that law. It begins with careful attention to precisely what Mishnah says, its concrete and specific words. Generalization comes much later and in different ways.

1. So what the Talmud means by "an explanation of the Mishnah" is this: to spell out the meanings of the words, the phrases, the sentences of the Mishnah. To explain the Mishnah, we ask about its sources. We interpret the meanings of unclear phrases. We ask obvious and compelling questions of concrete meaning.

But the Talmud is more things as well.

2. It explains the implications of the Mishnah's rule. The Talmud will want to take Mishnah's specific rule and turn it into something more general. The Mishnah may speak in concrete terms. The Talmud may tell us what those terms imply. The Mishnah may speak of a single case. The Talmud will want to tell us how the rule governing that case applies to other cases. In this regard, the three examples of Eliezer's opinion are suggestive. They show us how the Talmud will work (even though they are in the Mishnah) to make concrete and specific something general in Mishnah, or to make general and applicable to many things something concrete and specific in Mishnah.

In a way, you might say what the Talmud will do is what Mishnah leaves undone.

3. And the Talmud goes on, beyond the frontiers laid out by the Mishnah's treatment of a law, to explore important new ideas about that same law. The Talmud is given a topic or a theme by the Mishnah. The Talmud will work its way out to the limits of the theme as the Mishnah treats that theme.

Then the Talmud will go beyond those limits. It will treat the theme in new ways, in ways unimagined by the Mishnah. So there is a discipline, and there is a kind of freedom. The discipline is to explore fully what is said. The freedom is to use the imagination to treat the topic or theme in entirely new ways.

The discipline of the Talmud requires spelling out the meaning of, "There are no vows." The discipline, further, requires that we test our theory of what the Mishnah means against other things the Mishnah says, for instance, what Abbaye and Raba say against what Mishnah says. The discipline demands that we state the sources of the Mishnah, if we can think what they might be.

4. But the Talmud is free too. It is free to expand upon a subject. It has the right, when treating the topic of the Mishnah—namely, untying vows—to go on to a related matter. This second notion is that if one takes a vow not to derive benefit from someone, the vow, when untied, must be untied in the presence of that same person. That is an idea relevant to our Mishnah-passage. But it is not in our Mishnah-passage. Our Mishnah-passage does not require it. We should have fully and completely understood what Mishnah wants to tell us without knowing that fact.

It follows that the Talmud has freedom to move beyond the limits of the Mishnah's treatment of the Mishnah's theme.

It exercises other sorts of freedom as well. The *aggadic* tale about Zedekiah and Nebuchadnezzar surely exists on its own, as a condemnation of faithless sages, and not merely to serve our Talmudic discussion, let alone our Mishnah.

So the Talmud draws together many things in presenting what its author conceives to be the proper approach to the Mishnah. So we no longer can say merely, "explanation of the Mishnah."

TALMUD, TORAH, JUDAISM

Once more we ask what we have learned about Judaism. The answer is, Judaism is a religion about keeping your word because it speaks about ordinary, everyday circumstances, moments when you say something you later regret. The Torah wants to find a middle path between the holiness of your word and the reality of your life. One important concern of Judaism is to make us people who keep our word to God and to our fellow human beings. Another important interest is our own self-respect and self-esteem. A third is how we keep these two values in balance. The reason that the Talmud is important for Judaism today is that it teaches us how to think about problems that we create for ourselves through our power to express ourselves.

PART FOUR

The Talmud Speaks to Us about Deeds and Beliefs

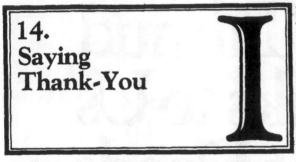

14. Saying Thank-You

MISHNAH BERAKHOT 6:1

In our first two passages of the Talmud, our attention was drawn to the traits of the Talmud itself: What to expect when we open the Talmud. How it explains and expands the Mishnah. For that purpose, we studied topics not familiar in our everyday religious life as Jews. We wanted to concentrate on the Talmud, rather than on what we learn from the Talmud for our own lives. I even claimed that the Talmud is not directly relevant to our everyday life, so that we could study the Talmud in the right spirit: to ask *its* questions—not necessarily ours—and to learn what *it* wants to say, not especially what we wanted to hear.

That gave us a chance to see the Talmud as Talmud and to ask about its traits and its character.

Now we will reverse ourselves and, both in this part and in Part Five, turn to passages in the Talmud that directly speak to us.

How does the Talmud lay out things that we as Jews already say and do? What is its mode of thinking and analyzing religious practices with which we are entirely familiar? Finally, what do we learn from the Talmud about things we already know? This is now the work of a new and ambitious passage. But, as you will see, the passage is not difficult.

The topic of the Talmud is the blessings that we say over food. Most Jews know that we say a blessing before we eat a piece of bread or drink a cup of wine. Indeed, one of the things nearly everyone learns in religious education is to say such a blessing. So the topic before us is familiar: blessings for food. But what will the Talmud want to know *about* that topic? What will it want to tell us that we do not know? Above all, what does it mean that we recite such blessings? What does it say about us and about our attitude toward the world and toward God? What conclusions should we reach?

Here is the main point: *We are what we do. But we do what we believe.* So how shall we learn, from what we do, what we believe? And how shall we describe what we are on the basis of what we believe and what we do?

These are deep questions. They touch the foundations of our humanness, of what it means to us to be Jews.

The Mishnah is going to surprise you because it is rather bland and merely tells us facts. It raises no problems. It is simply a repertoire of rules: What blessing you say for one thing, what blessing you say for some other thing. We have a question in No. 1. Then we are given three different things: (1) fruit of a tree, [No. 2]—except wine, [Nos. 3-4]; (2) fruit of the ground, [No. 5], except for bread, [Nos. 6-7]; and (3) vegetables, [No. 8]. We have a triplet: fruit of a tree, fruit of the ground, and vegetables.

Before proceeding, let us learn the Mishnah carefully. Try to memorize it (in Hebrew or in English) so you can understand its inner construction.

Try to understand how it is put together and why the person who put it together did it in this particular way. That is a familiar question for you, is it not?

1	How do they say a blessing over fruit?	כֵּיצַד מְבָרְכִין עַל הַפֵּרוֹת?
2	Over fruit of a tree, a person says [Blessed are you, Lord, our God, ruler of the world, who] creates fruit of the tree.	עַל פֵּרוֹת הָאִילָן הוּא אוֹמֵר „בּוֹרֵא פְּרִי הָעֵץ",
3	Except for wine, for	חוּץ מִן הַיַּיִן, שֶׁ
4	over wine, a person says [Blessed are you, Lord, our God, ruler of the world, who] creates fruit of the vine.	עַל הַיַּיִן הוּא אוֹמֵר „בּוֹרֵא פְּרִי הַגָּפֶן".
5	And over fruit of the ground a person says [Blessed are you, Lord, our God, ruler of the world, who] creates fruit of the ground.	וְעַל פֵּרוֹת הָאָרֶץ הוּא אוֹמֵר „בּוֹרֵא פְּרִי הָאֲדָמָה",

6	Except for bread, for	חוּץ מִן הַפַּת, שֶׁ
7	Over bread, a person says, [Blessed are you, Lord, our God, ruler of the world who] brings bread out of the earth.	עַל הַפַּת הוּא אוֹמֵר „הַמּוֹצִיא לֶחֶם מִן הָאָרֶץ״.
8	And over vegetables, a person says [Blessed are you, Lord our God, ruler of the world, who] creates fruit of the ground.	וְעַל הַיְרָקוֹת הוּא אוֹמֵר „בּוֹרֵא פְּרִי הָאֲדָמָה״.
9	Rabbi Judah says, [A person says, Blessed are you, Lord our God, ruler of the world, who] creates different kinds of seeds.	רַבִּי יְהוּדָה אוֹמֵר „בּוֹרֵא מִינֵי דְשָׁאִים״.

Vocabulary

how	כֵּיצַד	wine	יַיִן
bless	בֵּרַךְ	vine	גֶּפֶן
pieces of fruit	פֵּרוֹת	land	אֶרֶץ
on, for	עַל	ground	אֲדָמָה
tree	אִילָן	piece of bread	פַּת
he	הוּא	brings out	מוֹצִיא
creates	בּוֹרֵא	bread	לֶחֶם
tree	עֵץ	vegetables	יְרָקוֹת
except	חוּץ	kinds of seed	מִינֵי דְשָׁאִים
for, from	מִן		

he Mishnah-passage, as I told you, is remarkably easy to follow. It simply lists three different things people consume—fruit of a tree, fruit of the ground, and vegetables. In the time of the Mishnah, these were the things people ate daily. So it was natural for the author of the Mishnah to construct a poem in a triplet to give the blessing for these three things.

Notice the author takes for granted that you are acquainted with the proper formula for a blessing, which is:

Blessed are you, Lord our God, ruler of the world, who . . .

So the person who makes up our Mishnah takes for granted you know in advance what he is telling you. (1) You know what a blessing is. We ask, *How* do they say a blessing? (2) You know the basic formula for a blessing. We start, " . . . who."

You must therefore ask yourself, what is the real purpose of the person who made up this little poem? What does he want us to learn?

Could it be the exceptions of wine, then bread?

Could it be the disagreement of Judah in No. 9?

Is it not strange that the same blessing—"fruit of the ground"—applies to fruit of the ground and vegetables, things that grow in the ground and not on trees? Why does the Mishnah treat the two separately?

Why indeed, if not to allow Judah to give his quite different opinion? The only striking statement in the triplet is the one that breaks free of what has already been said, and that is No. 9.

This kind of questioning is interesting, but it does not bring us any closer to the Talmud.

The Talmud is going to be struck by something else entirely. It is going to have its own problem. That problem is in no way related to the simple explanations of the phrasing and wording of Mishnah that my questions are meant to call to your mind.

Yet even now, I think you can predict what the Talmud will want to know about our Mishnah-passage:

What is the source of this Mishnah?

But what will be explained is not the source of the formulas for the several different blessings. The Talmud will take for granted that that is not the most important question it can ask.

The Talmud wants to know what everyone should have already known:

Why do we have to say blessings at all?

Perhaps in our own time, when we are aware of the importance of nature and ecological balance, we do not find blessings so surprising. For what blessings say in a framework of holiness is what we try to do when we protect and watch over the natural environment—we revere the world God made and we want to protect it. We are grateful for what we have.

15. Explaining the Mishnah

The first thing to know is, What is the source of this rule? To understand what the Talmud thinks we should know, you must remember that meals conclude with the Blessing for Food, *Birkat hammazon*. What troubles the Talmud is this: Since we have to say a blessing *after* we eat, why do we—in addition—have to say a blessing *before* we eat?

When the Talmud asks, "What is the source of this rule?" it means the source of the rule that, before eating, we say a blessing over fruit of trees, fruit of the ground, and vegetables. This is not quite to the point of a Mishnah which asks, "*What* do we say?" But it is relevant.

A. What is the source of this rule?	מְנָא ה״מ (הָנֵי מִילֵּי)
B. As our rabbis have taught:	הְּתָנוּ רַבָּנָן
C. [The fruit thereof will be] holy, for giving praise to the Lord (Lev. 19:24).	(וְהָיָה כָּל פִּרְיוֹ) קֹדֶשׁ הִלּוּלִים לה׳
D. This teaches that they [pieces of produce] require a blessing before them and after them.	מְלַמֵּד שֶׁטְּעוּנִים בְּרָכָה לִפְנֵיהֶם וּלְאַחֲרֵיהֶם
E. On this basis did R. 'Aqiba say,	מִכָּאן אָמַר ר״ע (ר׳ עֲקִיבָא)
F. It is prohibited for a person to taste anything before he has said a blessing.	אָסוּר לָאָדָם שֶׁיִּטְעוֹם כְּלוּם קוֹדֶם שֶׁיְּבָרֵךְ

Vocabulary

What is the source of this rule?	מְנָא ה״מ (הָנֵי מֵילֵי)
they require	טְעוּנִים
blessing	בְּרָכָה
on this basis	מִכָּאן

hat is the nature of the proof? Not surprisingly, it is a citation of Scripture, Lev. 19:24. That verse refers to fruit of an orchard four years after the trees were planted. That "fruit of the fourth year" may not be eaten at all. The verse says that one must give praise to the Lord. Notice that the word for giving praise, *hillulim*, is plural. It means that there are two acts of giving praise to the Lord. (1) One comes after we eat. (2) The other comes before we eat.

It follows that we have to say a blessing before and after we eat these different sorts of produce.

It is exceedingly important that Aqiba's saying (E-F) is attached to the proof. For everything that follows in the Talmudic elaboration and discussion of our Mishnah-passage will develop Aqiba's basic idea.

It is simple. One must say a blessing before he or she eats anything. Aqiba says this in the negative. One is forbidden to taste anything before saying a blessing over it.

Have we explained the Mishnah-passage? In a way, we have filled it out rather than explained it. The Talmud finds most striking not *how* we bless these kinds of produce but *that* we must bless the food. And not that alone, but that the blessing is required in advance of eating that fruit, and not merely afterward (as everyone knows).

We wonder whether the Talmud is not explaining something that hardly requires explanation. The people who made up this passage know full well that we say the Blessing for Food, Grace after meals. They also know that we say the blessings listed in the Mishnah-passage. In fact, they want to know why we say blessings at all.

It would therefore appear that the Talmud really wants to talk about, in this *halakhic* passage, a matter of religious conviction: the recitation of blessings and the religious attitude required for saying them. And that is precisely why Aqiba's saying, and not Mishnah at all, will be subjected to extension and amplification. In point of fact, the Mishnah-passage will be forgotten in the Talmud that follows.

16. Expanding the Explanation

After some discussion that we shall bypass, the Talmud that serves our Mishnah-passage returns to this weighty saying of Aqiba: We cannot enjoy anything of this world without saying a blessing. In expanding our explanation of the Mishnah, we will say some deep things about ourselves as human beings and our relationship to God.

The Talmud will now do with Aqiba's saying in explanation of the Mishnah what we have seen the Talmud do with a Mishnah-passage itself. The Talmud will slowly and patiently unpack all the layers of meaning contained in that saying. It will consider each and every implication of what Aqiba has told us.

The first thing it will do is repeat the saying and then spell it out. Why, the Talmud will ask, should we not derive enjoyment from this world without saying a blessing over what gives us pleasure or benefit? Because what we are taking does not belong to us. We must at least admit and acknowledge that fact and express our thanks for what is given to us. That is the main point of the Talmudic passage before us.

A. Our rabbis have taught:	ת״ר
B. It is prohibited for a person to derive enjoyment from this world without a blessing.	אָסוּר לוֹ לְאָדָם שֶׁיֶּהֱנֶה מִן העוה״ז (הָעוֹלָם הַזֶּה) בְּלֹא בְרָכָה.
C. And all who derive enjoyment from this world without a blessing commit sacrilege.	וְכָל הַנֶּהֱנֶה מִן העוה״ז בְּלֹא בְרָכָה מָעַל.
D. What is the remedy [for such a person]?	מַאי תַקַּנְתֵּיהּ?
E. Let him go to a sage.	יֵלֵךְ אֵצֶל חָכָם.
F. Let him go to a sage?!	יֵלֵךְ אֵצֶל חָכָם,

G. What will he do for him?

מַאי עָבֵיד לֵיהּ?

H. Lo, he [already] has committed a violation.

הָא עָבֵיד לֵיהּ אִיסוּרָא.

I. But said Raba,

אֶלָּא אָמַר רָבָא

J. Let him go to a sage in the first place

יֵלֵךְ אֵצֶל חָכָם מֵעִיקָרָא

K. and he [the sage] will teach the person blessings,

וִילַמְּדֶנּוּ בְּרָכוֹת

L. so that he may not come into the grip of sacrilege.

שֶׁלֹּא יָבֹא לִידֵי מְעִילָה.

M. Said Rab Judah said Samuel,

אָמַר רַב יְהוּדָה אָמַר שְׁמוּאֵל

N. Whoever derives enjoyment from this world without a blessing is as if he derives benefit from Holy Things that belong to Heaven,

כָּל הַנֶּהֱנָה מִן העוה״ז בְּלֹא בְּרָכָה כְּאִילּוּ נֶהֱנָה מִקָּדְשֵׁי שָׁמַיִם

O. since it is said, The earth is the Lord's and the fulness thereof (Psalm 24:1).

שנא׳ לה׳ הָאָרֶץ וּמְלוֹאָהּ

P. R. Levi contrasted [two verses of Scripture]:

ר׳ לֵוִי רְמִי

Q. It is written, The earth is the Lord's and the fulness thereof (Psalm 24:1).

כְּתִיב לה׳ הָאָרֶץ וּמְלוֹאָהּ

R. And it is written, The heavens belong to the Lord, but the earth did he give to people. (Psalm 115:16).

וּכְתִיב הַשָּׁמַיִם שָׁמַיִם לה׳ וְהָאָרֶץ נָתַן לִבְנֵי אָדָם

S. There is no contradiction.

לָא קַשְׁיָא

T. The former verse applies before [one has said] a blessing; the latter verse applies after [one has said] a blessing.

כָּאן קוֹדֶם בְּרָכָה כָּאן לְאַחַר בְּרָכָה.

94

this world	הָעוה"ז (הָעוֹלָם הַזֶּה)
without	בְּלֹא
one who derives enjoyment	הַנֶּהֱנָה
commit sacrilege	מָעַל
what	מַאי
his remedy	תַּקַּנְתֵּיה
do	עֲבִיד
for him	לֵיה
violation	אִיסּוּרָא
in the first place	מֵעִיקָרָא
into the grip	לִידֵי
sacrilege	מְעִילָה
Holy Things that belong to Heaven	קָדְשֵׁי שָׁמַיִם
contrasted	רְמִי
contradiction	קַשְׁיָא
after	לְאַחַר

-C begins in Hebrew. If I gain benefit from anything in this world, I must say a blessing. Why? Because the fruits and vegetables of the world are the fruits of creation. God made, and continues to make, the world in such a way as to give me everything I need. God creates the world and all its blessings. Therefore, these things belong to God. I cannot enjoy God's belongings without thanks, and if I do, I misappropriate what is holy. That is (C), I commit sacrilege.

The passage now shifts to Aramaic. It will comment on what has gone before.

What should a person who actually eats an apple without a blessing do?

The answer to the question in D is E: Go to a sage. Why? Will the sage make up the blessing the person has not said?

No, the Talmud hastens to add. That is not the meaning of D-E. The Talmud does not speak in absurd statements, but it does want to work out its ideas slowly and in a clear way.

Go to a sage (F-H) for what purpose? Because, Raba says, a sage will teach you what to say (J-L). The point of it all is to return to our Mishnah. The sage will teach you the blessings you require. That is, the sage will teach you Mishnah-passages such as the one we learned at the outset.

What the Talmud has accomplished is not quite what we had expected. The Talmud began with Aqiba's saying that we cannot enjoy anything without saying a blessing. Now this led us far from the substance of our Mishnah-passage.

We learn (1) blessings in the Mishnah-passage. The Talmud then ignores what the Mishnah-passage has told us and turns to what the Mishnah-passage has not told us: (2) the purpose of blessings.

This troubled the person who developed A-C by adding D-L. And what that person did is clever. He has turned Aqiba's saying back upon itself and forced us to return to the *substance* of what Mishnah actually tells us.

So the Talmudic writer has taken what seemed (quite rightly, I think) a rather irrelevant approach to the explanation of Mishnah and turned it around so that it leads us back to the very lesson Mishnah wishes us to learn—the various blessings we recite.

This is impressive and artful, since on the face of it, all we have is a sequence of loosely related thoughts.

What follows are two further relevant expansions of this expansion of the explanation of Mishnah, M-O and P-T. There will be more beyond.

Judah's point in the name of Samuel is precisely what we already have said in C and again in K-L. Samuel raises the issue of sacrilege—deriving benefit from Holy Things, which belong to Heaven, that is, to God. What Samuel does is very simple: He provides a proof-text for that fundamental viewpoint.

The proof-text is good; it says that the whole earth belongs to God. That is the reason we say a blessing before deriving benefit from anything of this world.

Notice that the discussion is not quite what we should have expected after A-L. Samuel speaks of enjoying anything, while the principal interest up to now has been food or other sorts of natural produce. But the point is the same.

The second expansion of our expansion (P-T) takes up the preceding one. It is a sign of how carefully and sensibly our passage has been put together. Once we have heard Samuel's proof-text, relevant as it is to what has gone before, we proceed to develop further ideas about that proof-text.

Levi takes two verses that contradict one another. One says the earth belongs to God. The other says the earth belongs to the human race (Q and R). S declares there is no contradiction. And T makes the necessary point. The earth belongs to the Lord—until we say a blessing. Once we have said a blessing, God gives the earth to the human race. This shows the main point in a different and engaging way. It is the reason we must say a blessing *before* we eat a piece of fruit as well as afterward.

The same points will now be repeated in yet other ways, as the Talmud runs its course.

17. Expanding the Expansion

The author of the passage we just learned was struck by the contrast between two scriptural passages that seem to say opposite things. He solves that problem by showing that the opposition is not a contradiction but refers to different points in time or different circumstances. One verse refers to the time before one has said a blessing. Then the earth is the Lord's. Another verse refers to the time after one has said a blessing, when God has given earth to humanity.

This mode of thought naturally invites other sorts of contrasts between two or more Scriptural verses. The supposed contradiction may be solved by reference to different times or different situations.

Once we have introduced a mode of thinking about a given problem, we can apply that mode to other problems. The problem of the importance of saying blessings leads to the view that we must say blessings when we derive benefit from any natural advantage. We contrast verses to underline the importance of saying blessings. Now what do we do?

We contrast other verses and make points not directly relevant to the particular problem we have been discussing—saying blessings. Yet, as we shall see, what is said is relevant in general, if not in particular. We never fully abandon the line of thought we began so long ago. We just move along its path, not bound by its own direction, exploring its highways and byways.

A. Said R. Hanina bar Papa,	א״ר חֲנִינָא בַּר פָּפָּא,
B. Whoever derives enjoyment from this world without a blessing	כָּל הַנֶּהֱנָה מִן הָעוה״ז בְּלֹא בְרָכָה,
C. is as if he steals from the Holy One blessed be he, and from the community of Israel,	כְּאִילוּ גּוֹזֵל להקב״ה (לְהַקָּדוֹשׁ בָּרוּךְ הוּא) וּכְנֶסֶת יִשְׂרָאֵל,
D. since it is said, Whoever	שנא׳ גּוֹזֵל

robs his father or his mother and says, It is no transgression—that person is a companion of a destroyer (Prov. 28:24).

אָבִיו וְאִמּוֹ, וְאוֹמֵר אֵין פָּשַׁע, חָבֵר הוּא לְאִישׁ מַשְׁחִית.

E. And "his father" refers only to the Holy One, blessed be he, as it is said,

וְאֵין אָבִיו אֶלָּא הקב״ה (הַקָּדוֹשׁ בָּרוּךְ הוּא) שנא'

F. Is not he your father, who has gotten you (Deut. 32:6).

הֲלֹא הוּא אָבִיךָ קָנֶךָ.

G. And mother refers only to the community of Israel,

וְאֵין אִמּוֹ אֶלָּא כְּנֶסֶת יִשְׂרָאֵל,

H. since it is said, Hear my son, the instruction of your father, and do not forsake the teaching of your mother (Prov. 1:8).

שנא' שְׁמַע בְּנִי מוּסַר אָבִיךָ וְאַל תִּטּוֹשׁ תּוֹרַת אִמֶּךָ.

I. What [is the meaning of the phrase], That person is a companion of a destroyer?

מַאי חָבֵר הוּא לְאִישׁ מַשְׁחִית?

J. Said R. Hanina b. Papa,

א״ר חֲנִינָא בַּר פָּפָּא,

K. he is a companion of Jeroboam, the son of Nabat,

חָבֵר הוּא לְיָרָבְעָם בֶּן נְבָט

L. who destroyed Israel for their Father in heaven.

שֶׁהִשְׁחִית אֶת יִשְׂרָאֵל לַאֲבִיהֶם שֶׁבַּשָּׁמַיִם.

Vocabulary

he steals	גּוֹזֵל
community	כְּנֶסֶת
the Holy One, blessed be he	הקב״ה (הַקָּדוֹשׁ בָּרוּךְ הוּא)
companion	חָבֵר
he destroyed	הִשְׁחִית

-C repeats the earlier main point. Deriving enjoyment from something of this world without saying a blessing is like stealing from God. But, Hanina adds, it is also like stealing from the community of Israel.

Now Hanina offers a sequence of proof texts. Robbing one's father (D) is the first. E then proves that "father" means God, and F is an appropriate proof. Then we come to the community of Israel (W). G-H explain how Scripture proves that "mother" means Community of Israel. The verse cited in D refers to a companion of a destroyer, and we should explain that odd phrase. So I raises the question. That is, we have a second-level explanation of a first-level explanation of our *original* proposition. To put matters graphically: our original proposition is A-C. This then is worked out and explained by D-H. Then elements of D-H have to be explained, and that is completed by I-L.

Our passage is *midrash aggadah*. It is *aggadah* because it deals with beliefs, rather than concrete practices. It is *midrash* because it involves a search (from the root *darash*) of Scripture. *Midrash aggadah* is the explanation of *aggadic* passages of Scripture. There is a second kind of *midrash*, *midrash halakhah*, which explains *halakhic* passages of Scripture such as the laws we find in Exodus, Leviticus, Numbers, and Deuteronomy.

At this point, the expansion of the Talmud's expansion of its explanation of Mishnah is complete. We turn, then, to an essay expanding the expansion.

M. R. Hanina b. Papa contrasted [two Scriptural verses]:	ר׳ חֲנִינָא בַּר פָּפָּא רְמִי,
N. It is written, Therefore will I take back my grain in the time thereof (Hosea 2:11).	כְּתִיב וְלָקַחְתִּי דְנָנִי בְּעִתּוֹ וגו׳ (וְגוֹמֵר),
O. And it is written, And you shall gather in your corn (Deut. 11:14).	וּכְתִיב וְאָסַפְתָּ דְגָנֶךָ וגו׳,

P. There is no contradiction.

Q. The latter verse refers to the time in which Israel does the will of the Omnipresent.

R. The former verse refers to the time in which Israel does not carry out the will of the Omnipresent.

ל״ק (לָא קַשְׁיָא).

כָּאן

בִּזְמַן שֶׁיִּשְׂרָאֵל עוֹשִׂין רְצוֹנוֹ שֶׁל מָקוֹם,

כָּאן

בִּזְמַן שֶׁאֵין יִשְׂרָאֵל עוֹשִׂין רְצוֹנוֹ שֶׁל מָקוֹם.

Vocabulary

there is no contradiction	ל״ק (לָא קַשְׁיָא)
will	רָצוֹן
the Omnipresent	מָקוֹם

Each verse, in its own context, makes sense, but when they are put together, they contradict one another. Hanina, however, makes an interesting contrast between times of plenty and times of need.

We know from the second paragraph of the *Shema'*, that when the Jewish people obey God's commandments, things go well; and when they do not, things go badly.

If you will earnestly heed the commandments I give you this day, to love the Lord your God and to serve Him with all your heart and soul, then I will favor your land with rain at the proper season . . . and you will have an ample harvest of grain and wine and oil . . . Take care lest you be tempted to forsake God and turn to false gods in worship. For then the wrath of the Lord will be directed against you. He will close the heavens and hold back the rain. The earth will not yield its produce.

Hanina makes the same point in striking language.

101

When Israel, the Jewish people, does the will of God, then you shall gather in corn. When Israel, the Jewish people, does not carry out the will of God, then "I will take back my grain."

We have not strayed far from the original point—that we must say blessings. Saying a blessing is a way of expressing our thanks to God. Then God gives us what belongs to God. If we do not say a blessing, God does not give us what is not ours. When Israel does God's will, the grain belongs to Israel. When Israel does not do God's will, the grain remains God's.

We now return to "gathering in grain," which has yet another meaning. "Gathering grain" is something we do by working for a living. So when we speak of "gathering in grain," we also may mean work and earn a living, support yourself (and, in time to come, your family).

The rabbis of the Mishnah and the Talmud considered working for a living as something one did *instead* of studying and teaching Torah. They were not paid for their work as rabbis, as disciples and teachers of Torah. They made a living as farmers or craftsmen. Does Scripture tell people to gather in grain, work for a living *rather* than study Torah? That would be an amazing message, and it is the subject of the next section of our Talmud.

A. Our rabbis have taught:	תּ״ר
B. And you will gather in your grain.	וְאָסַפְתָּ דְגָנֶךְ
C. What does Scripture teach?	מַה תּ״ל (תַּלְמוּד לוֹמַר)?
D. Since it is said, This book of the law will not depart from your mouth (Joshua 1:8),	לְפִי שֶׁנֶּא׳ לֹא יָמוּשׁ סֵפֶר הַתּוֹרָה הַזֶּה מִפִּיךָ.
E. one might have thought that these things are to be just as they are written.	יָכוֹל דְּבָרִים כִּכְתָבָן.
F. Scripture therefore says, You will gather in your grain.	תּ״ל וְאָסַפְתָּ דְגָנֶךְ,
G. [This means] combine with them a worldly occupation,	הַנְהֵג בָּהֶן מִנְהַג דֶּרֶךְ אֶרֶץ,

H. the words of R. Ishmael.

I. R. Simeon b. Yohai says,

J. Is it possible for a person to plough in the time of ploughing,

K. sow in the time of sowing,

L. harvest in the time of harvesting,

M. thresh in the time of threshing,

N. winnow in the time of the wind—

O. [if so]—as to the Torah, what ever will become of it?

P. But when Israel does the will of the Omnipresent,

Q. their work is done by others,

R. since it is said, And strangers shall stand and feed your flocks (Isaiah 61:5).

S. And when Israel does not do the will of the Omnipresent,

T. their work is done by their own hands,

U. as it is said, And you will gather in your grain.

V. and not only so, but

W. the work of other people is done by them [as well],

X. as it is said, And you will serve your enemy (Deut. 28:48).

דִּבְרֵי ר׳ יִשְׁמָעֵאל.

ר״ש (ר׳ שִׁמְעוֹן) בֶּן יוֹחַי אוֹמֵר,
אֶפְשָׁר אָדָם חוֹרֵשׁ בִּשְׁעַת חֲרִישָׁה,

חוֹרֵעַ בִּשְׁעַת זְרִיעָה,

וְקוֹצֵר בִּשְׁעַת קְצִירָה,

וְדָשׁ בִּשְׁעַת דִּישָׁה,

וְזוֹרֶה בִּשְׁעַת הָרוּחַ

תּוֹרָה
מַה תְּהֵא עָלֶיהָ?

אֶלָּא בִּזְמַן שֶׁיִּשְׂרָאֵל עוֹשִׂין רְצוֹנוֹ שֶׁל מָקוֹם,

מְלַאכְתָּן נַעֲשִׂית ע״י (עַל יְדֵי) אֲחֵרִים,

שנא׳ וְעָמְדוּ זָרִים וְרָעוּ צֹאנְכֶם וגו׳.

וּבִזְמַן שֶׁאֵין יִשְׂרָאֵל עוֹשִׂין רְצוֹנוֹ שֶׁל מָקוֹם,

מְלַאכְתָּן נַעֲשִׂית ע״י עַצְמָן,

שנא׳ וְאָסַפְתָּ דְגָנֶךָ.

וְלֹא עוֹד אֶלָּא

שֶׁמְּלֶאכֶת אֲחֵרִים נַעֲשִׂית עַל יָדָן,

שנא׳ וְעָבַדְתָּ אֶת אוֹיְבֶיךָ וגו׳.

V. A. Said Abbaye,	אָמַר אַבַּיֵי
B. Many did things in accord with R. Ishmael,	הַרְבֵּה עָשׂוּ כְּרַבִּי יִשְׁמָעֵאל
C. and it worked out for them.	וְעָלְתָה בְּיָדָן,
D. [Others did things] in accord with R. Simeon b. Yohai,	כר' שִׁמְעוֹן בֶּן יוֹחָי
E. and it did not work out for them.	וְלֹא עָלְתָה בְּיָדָן.
F. Said Raba to rabbis,	א״ל רָבָא לְרַבָּנָן,
G. By your leave,	בְּמָטוּתָא מִינַיְיכוּ
H. in the days of Nisan and in the days of Tishre	בְּיוֹמֵי נִיסָן וּבְיוֹמֵי תִּשְׁרֵי
I. do not appear before me,	לָא תִּתְחֲזוּ קַמַּאי,
J. so that you may not be anxious about your food	כִּי הֵיכִי דְּלָא תִּטְרְדוּ בִּמְזוֹנַיְיכוּ
K. for the entire year.	כּוּלָא שַׁתָּא.

Vocabulary

What does Scripture teach?	מַה ת״ל (תַּלְמוּד לוֹמַר)	it worked out for them	עָלְתָה בְּיָדָן
just as they are written	כִּכְתָבָן	by your leave	בְּמָטוּתָא מִנַיְיכוּ
worldly occupation	דֶּרֶךְ אֶרֶץ	in the days of	כְּיוֹמֵי
plow	חוֹרֵשׁ	[the month of] Nisan	נִיסָן
sow	זוֹרֵעַ	[the month of] Tishre	תִּשְׁרֵי
harvest	קוֹצֵר	you appear	תִּתְחֲזוּ
thresh	דָּשׁ	before me	קַמַּאי
winnow	זוֹרֶה	so that	כִּי הֵיכִי
is done	נַעֲשִׂית	be anxious	תִּטְרְדוּ
by	ע״י (עַל יְדֵי)	your food	מְזוֹנַיְיכוּ
their own hands	עַצְמָן	for the entire year	כּוּלָא שַׁתָּא

If we are told to gather in grain, why does Scripture also say to spend our time in Torah study (D)? We might have the notion that we should do nothing but study Torah. Therefore, F says, we have to be told to gather in grain as well. R. Ishmael's view is that one should both work for a living and study Torah.

Simeon b. Yohai asks a disturbing question (I-O). If you work for a living, when will you ever find time to study Torah? His answer is that doing God's will is the important thing. Simeon b. Yohai's reading, of course, brings us back to the verse with which we began (U). He carries to its logical extreme the simple claim that the earth belongs to God, but if we say a blessing, God gives it to us.

Simeon maintains that if God really owns the earth, and if we do what God wants, then God will take care of us. Simeon sees that promise in a concrete way. We shall not even have to work.

This is an extreme interpretation of the belief that God blesses us—for instance, with rain—when we do God's will. The *Shema* says that. It is a radical claim that when you do God's will, "You will gather in grain." Ishmael takes a more even-handed position. But Simeon, moving out to the extremes of the world-view of the Talmud, teaches us something still more important. Simeon believes that when you set one foot into a system, you can never stop until you have walked through all the highways and byways of that system.

Perhaps this mode of thinking seems far-fetched to you. You probably don't know anyone who wonders about finding a balance between work and play, between learning and doing. Yet there is balance in your lives. Part of the time you play, part of the time you study, and there are other things you do with your life. If you are fortunate, you may have music lessons, or you may be active in sports. Since you're reading this book, you take a certain amount of time off and use it to study Torah, just as the rabbis say. In these ways, you seek a balance among the many different things you want and are expected to do.

That is why Abbaye says that people who did what Ishmael says, balance earning a living with studying Torah, did all right. People who took the extreme, idealistic advice of Simeon and only studied and kept the teachings of the Torah did not do well. Abbaye's point is that, in the end, we have a right to test the advice of the great masters of the Torah against the practical results of their teachings.

The passage ends with an example of how Raba, like Abbaye, agrees with Ishmael. He told his students to go home during the planting and harvest seasons so that they could provide food for themselves and their families. During those months they should earn their living. Then they will study Torah the rest of the year.

So Abbaye and Raba deny that if one only studies Torah, then other people will support the Jewish people and do their work for them. This is a kind of teaching, Abbaye says, that we can test against the realities of the world. And when we do test it, we find it is wrong.

That is one viewpoint. Now let us hear the other. Along comes someone who agrees with Simeon b. Yohai and who criticizes Abbaye and Raba.

II. A. Said Rabbah b. Bar Hana, said R. Yohanan, in the name of R. Judah b. R. Ilai,	אָמַר רַבָּה בַּר בַּר חַנָה א״ר יוֹחָנָן מִשּׁוּם רַבִּי יְהוּדָה בר׳ אִלְעָאי,
B. Come and see:	בֹּא וּרְאֵה
C. Not like the olden generations are the newer generations.	שֶׁלֹּא כַּדּוֹרוֹת הָרִאשׁוֹנִים דוֹרוֹת הָאַחֲרוֹנִים.
D. In the olden generations, they made their study of Torah their fixed concern,	דוֹרוֹת הָרִאשׁוֹנִים עָשׂוּ תּוֹרָתָן קֶבַע
E. and their vocation their hobby,	וּמְלַאכְתָּן עֲרַאי,
F. both this and that worked out for them.	זוֹ וָזוֹ נִתְקַיְּימָה בְּיָדָן.
G. But the newer generations,	דוֹרוֹת הָאַחֲרוֹנִים
H. who made their vocation their fixed concern,	שֶׁעָשׂוּ מְלַאכְתָּן קֶבַע

106

I. and their study of Torah	וְתוֹרָתָן
their hobby—	עֲרַאי,
J. neither one nor the other	זוֹ וְזוֹ לֹא
worked out for them.	נִתְקַיְּימָה בְּיָדָן.

Vocabulary

the olden generations	דּוֹרוֹת הָרִאשׁוֹנִים
the newer generations	דּוֹרוֹת הָאַחֲרוֹנִים
fixed concern	קֶבַע
hobby	עֲרַאי
worked out for them	נִתְקַיְּימָה בְּיָדָן

abbah b. Bar Hana cites a saying that goes back to Judah b. R. Ilai, who lived at the same time as Simeon b. Yohai. And Judah says almost the same thing as Simeon. In olden days people studied most of the time and worked for a living part-time. They became good Torah students and made a proper living. In the newer generation, people worked to support themselves and their families most of the time and made Torah study a hobby. They did not make a good living, and didn't learn much.

The person who attached Judah b. R. Ilai's saying to Abbaye's and Raba's approval of Ishmael's advice certainly has something in mind, too. If people do what Raba and Abbaye say, things will not work out well.

So the issue stands.

107

18. The Talmud All Together

BABYLONIAN TALMUD BERAKHOT 35A-B (EXCERPT)

We now review the pieces of the Talmud together as a whole. What do we want to see? Our problem is different from before. The Talmud we now study is more wide-ranging. Its path has twists and turns. The Talmud's explanation of the Mishnah is, in this case, not its principal concern. Rather, the Talmud takes a winding road, and our job is to find out whether or not it is a single road.

Earlier, I argued that the Talmud is carefully put together. Someone gave much thought about how to organize the materials logically and in an interesting way. Now you have every right to challenge that opinion on the basis of what you have reviewed.

You must wonder about the validity of two opinions:

1. The Talmud explains the Mishnah.
2. The Talmud is a single, whole essay.

You have every right to conclude that the Talmud really is not interested in the Mishnah, and that the Talmud is just a strung-together mass of separate and distinct bits of thought—sayings, stories, *midrash aggadah, midrash-halakhah.*

As you reread the Talmudic passage we have studied (excerpts of the materials on Babylonian Talmud Berakhot 35a-b), see whether you can understand the logic of the person who put these things together. Do you see a purpose in the sequence of ideas and topics? More important, do you see a connection between one idea and the next, and is there a coherence of the whole?

These are the critical questions for the next exercise. First, we review the whole as we have seen it—phrase by phrase—but now complete.

| 1 | How do they say a blessing over fruit? | כֵּיצַד מְבָרְכִין עַל הַפֵּרוֹת? |

108

2	Over fruit of a tree, a person says [Blessed are you, Lord, our God, ruler of the world, who] creates fruit of the tree.	עַל פֵּרוֹת הָאִילָן הוּא אוֹמֵר „בּוֹרֵא פְּרִי הָעֵץ",
3	Except for wine, for	חוּץ מִן הַיַּיִן, שֶׁ
4	over wine, a person says [Blessed are you, Lord, our God, ruler of the world, who] creates fruit of the vine.	עַל הַיַּיִן הוּא אוֹמֵר „בּוֹרֵא פְּרִי הַגָּפָן".
5	And over fruit of the ground a person says [Blessed are you, Lord, our God, ruler of the world, who] creates fruit of the ground.	וְעַל פֵּרוֹת הָאָרֶץ הוּא אוֹמֵר „בּוֹרֵא פְּרִי הָאֲדָמָה",
6	Except for bread, for	חוּץ מִן הַפַּת, שֶׁ
7	Over bread, a person says, [Blessed are you, Lord, our God, ruler of the world who] brings bread out of the earth.	עַל הַפַּת הוּא אוֹמֵר „הַמּוֹצִיא לֶחֶם מִן הָאָרֶץ".
8	And over vegetables, a person says [Blessed are you, Lord our God, ruler of the world, who] creates fruit of the ground.	וְעַל הַיְרָקוֹת הוּא אוֹמֵר „בּוֹרֵא פְּרִי הָאֲדָמָה".

9	Rabbi Judah says,	רַבִּי יְהוּדָה אוֹמֵר
	[A person says, Blessed are you, Lord our God, ruler of the world, who] creates different kinds of seeds.	„בּוֹרֵא מִינֵי דְשָׁאִים".

I.	A.	What is the source of this rule?	מְנָא ה"מ (הָנֵי מִילֵי)?
	B.	As our rabbis have taught:	דְּתָנוּ רַבָּנָן,
	C.	[The fruit thereof will be] holy, for giving praise to the Lord (Lev. 19:24).	(יִהְיֶה כָּל פִּרְיוֹ) קֹדֶשׁ הִלּוּלִים לה'.
	D.	This teaches that they [pieces of produce] require a blessing before them and after them.	מְלַמֵּד, שֶׁטְעוּנִים בְּרָכָה לְפָנֵיהֶם וּלְאַחֲרֵיהֶם.
	E.	On this basis did R. 'Aqiba say,	מִכָּאן אָמַר ר"ע (ר' עֲקִיבָא),
	F.	It is prohibited for a person to taste anything before he has said a blessing.	אָסוּר לָאָדָם שֶׁיִּטְעוֹם כְּלוּם קוֹדֶם שֶׁיְּבָרֵךְ.

II.	A.	Our rabbis have taught:	ת"ר
	B.	It is prohibited for a person to derive enjoyment from this world without a blessing.	אָסוּר לוֹ לָאָדָם שֶׁיֵּהָנֶה מִן העוה"ז (הָעוֹלָם הַזֶּה) כְּלֹא בְּרָכָה.
	C.	And all who derive enjoyment from this world without a blessing commit sacrilege.	וְכָל הַנֶּהֱנֶה מִן העוה"ז בְּלֹא בְּרָכָה מָעַל.
	D.	What is the remedy [for such a person]?	מַאי תַּקַּנְתֵּיהּ?
	E.	Let him go to a sage.	יֵלֵךְ אֵצֶל חָכָם.
	F.	Let him go to a sage?!	יֵלֵךְ אֵצֶל חָכָם,
	G.	What will he do for him?	מַאי עָבִיד לֵיהּ?

H. Lo, he [already] has committed a violation.

I. But said Raba,

J. Let him go to a sage in the first place

K. and he [the sage] will teach the person blessings,

L. so that he may not come into the grip of sacrilege.

M. Said Rab Judah said Samuel,

N. Whoever derives enjoyment from this world without a blessing is as if he derives benefit from Holy Things that belong to Heaven,

O. since it is said, The earth is the Lord's and the fulness thereof (Psalm 24:1).

P. R. Levi contrasted [two verses of Scripture]:

Q. It is written, The earth is the Lord's and the fulness thereof [Psalm 24:1].

R. And it is written, The heavens belong to the Lord, but the earth did he give to people. (Psalm 115:16).

S. There is no contradiction.

T. The former verse applies before [one has said] a blessing, the latter verse applies after [one has said] a blessing.

הָא עָבִיד לֵיהּ אִיסוּרָא.

אֶלָּא אָמַר רָכָא

יֵלַךְ אֵצֶל חָכָם מֵעִיקָרָא

וִילַמְּדֶנּוּ בְּרָכוֹת

שֶׁלֹּא יָבֹא לִידֵי מְעִילָה.

אָמַר רַב יְהוּדָה אָמַר שְׁמוּאֵל

כָּל הַנֶּהֱנָה מִן
העוה״ז בְּלֹא בְּרָכָה כְּאִילוּ
נֶהֱנָה מִקָּדְשֵׁי שָׁמַיִם

שנא׳ לה׳ הָאָרֶץ וּמְלוֹאָהּ

ר׳ לֵוִי רְמִי

כְּתִיב לה׳ הָאָרֶץ וּמְלוֹאָהּ

וּכְתִיב הַשָּׁמַיִם
שָׁמַיִם לה׳ וְהָאָרֶץ
נָתַן לִבְנֵי אָדָם

לָא קַשְׁיָא
כָּאן קוֹדֶם בְּרָכָה
כָּאן לְאַחַר בְּרָכָה.

111

III. A. Said R. Hanina bar Papa,

B. Whoever derives enjoyment from this world without a blessing

C. is as if he steals from the Holy One blessed be he, and from the community of Israel,

D. since it is said, Whoever robs his father or his mother and says, It is no transgression—that person is a companion of a destroyer (Prov. 28:24).

E. And "his father" refers only to the Holy One, blessed be he, as it is said,

F. Is not he your father, who has gotten you (Deut. 32:6).

G. And mother refers only to the community of Israel,

H. since it is said, Hear my son, the instruction of your father, and do not forsake the teaching of your mother (Prov. 1:8).

I. What [is the meaning of the phrase], That person is a companion of a destroyer?

J. Said R. Hanina b. Papa,

K. he is a companion of Jeroboam, the son of Nabat,

L. who destroyed Israel for their Father in heaven.

א"ר חֲנִינָא בַּר פָּפָא,

כָּל הַנֶּהֱנֶה מִן העוה"ז בְּלֹא בְרָכָה,

כְּאִילוּ גוֹזֵל

להקב"ה (לְהַקָּדוֹשׁ בָּרוּךְ הוּא) וּכְנֶסֶת יִשְׂרָאֵל,

שנא' גוֹזֵל אָבִיו וְאִמּוֹ,

וְאוֹמֵר אֵין פָּשַׁע,

חָבֵר הוּא לְאִישׁ מַשְׁחִית.

וְאֵין אָבִיו אֶלָּא הקב"ה (הַקָּדוֹשׁ בָּרוּךְ הוּא) שנא'

הֲלֹא הוּא אָבִיךָ קָּנֶךָ.

וְאֵין אִמּוֹ אֶלָּא כְּנֶסֶת יִשְׂרָאֵל,

שנא' שְׁמַע בְּנִי מוּסַר אָבִיךָ וְאַל תִּטּוֹשׁ תּוֹרַת אִמֶּךָ.

מַאי חָבֵר הוּא לְאִישׁ מַשְׁחִית?

א"ר חֲנִינָא בַּר פָּפָא, חָבֵר הוּא לְירָבְעָם בֶּן נְבָט שֶׁהִשְׁחִית אֶת יִשְׂרָאֵל לַאֲבִיהֶם שֶׁבַּשָּׁמַיִם.

M. R. Hanina b. Papa contrasted [two Scriptural verses]:

ר׳ חֲנִינָא בַּר פָּפָא רָמֵי,

N. It is written, Therefore will I take back my grain in the time thereof.... (Hosea 2:11).

כְּתִיב וְלָקַחְתִּי דְגָנִי בְּעִתּוֹ וגו׳ (וְנוֹמַר),

O. And it is written, And you shall gather in your corn .... (Deut. 11:14).

וּכְתִיב וְאָסַפְתָּ דְגָנֶךְ וגו׳,

P. There is no contradiction.

ל״ק (לָא קַשְׁיָא).

Q. The latter verse refers to the time in which Israel does the will of the Omnipresent.

כָּאן בִּזְמַן שֶׁיִּשְׂרָאֵל עוֹשִׂין רְצוֹנוֹ שֶׁל מָקוֹם,

R. The former verse refers to the time in which Israel does not carry out the will of the Omnipresent.

כָּאן בִּזְמַן שֶׁאֵין יִשְׂרָאֵל עוֹשִׂין רְצוֹנוֹ שֶׁל מָקוֹם.

IV. A. Our rabbis have taught:

ת״ר

B. And you will gather in your grain.

וְאָסַפְתָּ דְגָנֶךְ

C. What does Scripture teach?

מַה ת״ל (תַּלְמוּד לוֹמַר)?

D. Since it is said, This book of the law will not depart from your mouth (Joshua 1:8),

לְפִי שֶׁנֶּא׳ לֹא יָמוּשׁ סֵפֶר הַתּוֹרָה הַזֶּה מִפִּיךָ.

E. one might have thought that these things are to be just as they are written.

יָכוֹל דְּבָרִים כִּכְתָבָן.

F. Scripture therefore says, You will gather in your grain.

ת״ל וְאָסַפְתָּ דְגָנֶךְ,

G. [This means] combine with them a worldly occupation,

הַנְהֵג בָּהֶן מִנְהַג דֶּרֶךְ אֶרֶץ,

H. the words of R. Ishmael.

I. R. Simeon b. Yohai says,

J. Is it possible for a person to plough in the time of ploughing,

K. sow in the time of sowing,

L. harvest in the time of harvesting,

M. thresh in the time of threshing,

N. winnow in the time of the wind—

O. [if so]—as to the Torah, what ever will become of it?

P. But when Israel does the will of the Omnipresent,

Q. their work is done by others,

R. since it is said, And strangers shall stand and feed your flocks (Isaiah 61:5).

S. And when Israel does not do the will of the Omnipresent,

T. their work is done by their own hands,

U. as it is said, And you will gather in your grain.

V. and not only so, but

W. the work of other people is done by them [as well],

X. as it is said, And you will serve your enemy (Deut. 28:48).

דִּבְרֵי ר׳ יִשְׁמָעֵאל.

ר״ש (ר׳ שִׁמְעוֹן) בֶּן יוֹחַי אוֹמֵר,

אֶפְשָׁר אָדָם חוֹרֵשׁ בִּשְׁעַת חֲרִישָׁה,

וְזוֹרֵעַ בִּשְׁעַת זְרִיעָה,

וְקוֹצֵר בִּשְׁעַת קְצִירָה,

וְדָשׁ בִּשְׁעַת דִּישָׁה,

וְזוֹרֶה בִּשְׁעַת הָרוּחַ

תּוֹרָה מַה תְּהֵא עָלֶיהָ?

אֶלָּא בִּזְמַן שֶׁיִּשְׂרָאֵל עוֹשִׂין רְצוֹנוֹ שֶׁל מָקוֹם,

מְלַאכְתָּן נַעֲשִׂית ע״י (עַל יְדֵי) אֲחֵרִים,

שֶׁנֶּא׳ וְעָמְדוּ זָרִים וְרָעוּ צֹאנְכֶם וכו׳.

וּבִזְמַן שֶׁאֵין יִשְׂרָאֵל עוֹשִׂין רְצוֹנוֹ שֶׁל מָקוֹם,

מְלַאכְתָּן נַעֲשִׂית ע״י עַצְמָן,

שֶׁנֶּא׳ וְאָסַפְתָּ דְגָנֶךָ.

וְלֹא עוֹד אֶלָּא שֶׁמְּלֶאכֶת אֲחֵרִים נַעֲשִׂית עַל יָדָן,

שֶׁנֶּא׳ וְעָבַדְתָּ אֶת אֹיְבֶיךָ וכו׳.

V. A. Said Abbaye,

B. Many did things in accord with R. Ishmael,

C. and it worked out for them.

D. [Others did things] in accord with R. Simeon b. Yohai,

E. and it did not work out for them.

F. Said Raba to rabbis,

G. By your leave,

H. in the days of Nisan and in the days of Tishre

I. do not appear before me,

J. so that you may not be anxious about your food

K. for the entire year.

VI. A. Said Rabbah b. Bar Hana, said R. Yohanan, in the name of R. Judah b. R. Ilai,

B. Come and see:

C. Not like the olden generations are the newer generations.

D. In the olden generations, they made their study of Torah their fixed concern,

E. and their vocation their hobby,

F. both this and that worked out for them.

G. But the newer generations,

אָמַר אַבַּיֵי

הַרְבֵּה עָשׂוּ

כְּרַבִּי יִשְׁמָעֵאל

וְעָלְתָה בְּיָדָן,

כר׳ שִׁמְעוֹן בֶּן יוֹחַי

וְלֹא עָלְתָה בְּיָדָן.

א״ל רָבָא לְרַבָּנָן,

בְּמָטוּתָא מִנַּיְיכוּ

בְּיוֹמֵי נִיסָן

וּבְיוֹמֵי תִּשְׁרֵי

לָא תִּתְחֲזוּ קַמַּאי,

כִּי הֵיכִי דְלָא

תִּטָּרְדוּ בִּמְזוֹנַיְיכוּ

כּוּלָא שַׁתָּא.

אָמַר רַבָּה בַּר בַּר חַנָה

א״ר יוֹחָנָן מִשּׁוּם רַבִּי

יְהוּדָה בר׳ אִלְעַאי,

בָּא וּרְאֵה

שֶׁלֹּא כַדּוֹרוֹת הָרִאשׁוֹנִים

דּוֹרוֹת הָאַחֲרוֹנִים.

דּוֹרוֹת הָרִאשׁוֹנִים

עָשׂוּ תּוֹרָתָן

קֶבַע

וּמְלַאכְתָּן

עֲרַאי,

זוֹ וְזוֹ נִתְקַיְימָה

בְּיָדָן.

דּוֹרוֹת הָאַחֲרוֹנִים

H. who made their vocation
their fixed concern,

I. and their study of Torah
their hobby—

J. neither one nor the other
worked out for them.

שֶׁעָשׂוּ מְלַאכְתָּן
קֶבַע
וְתוֹרָתָן
עֲרַאי,
זוֹ וָזוֹ לֹא
נִתְקַיְּמָה בְּיָדָן.

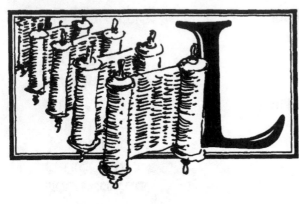et us rapidly review the sequence of units.

1. Mishnah: How do we bless?

2. Talmud: How do we know (that we say a blessing before we eat fruit, as well as afterward)?

3. It is prohibited to enjoy anything of this world without saying a blessing.

4. Whoever enjoys anything of this world without saying a blessing is as if he or she steals from God.

Concluding: You will gather in your grain.

5. Should one work at a worldly occupation or only study Torah?

If you see things this way, at what point do we have a problem?

It appears that the person who constructed our Talmud left us a problem in No. 5: What is the connection between 1-4, which is fairly coherent, and the issue of working for a living rather than always studying Torah? Indeed, Torah study is not even *mentioned* previously.

Why is Torah study relevant to (1) saying blessings and (2) expressing our thanks for God's blessings to us?

Before we proceed, let us read the Talmud as it is printed. This exercise will help us in two ways. First of all, it will show us what the Talmud looks like in its own setting. Second, it will allow us, once again, to think about the sequences of themes and ideas that make up this curious construction.

כיצד מברכין על הפירות על פירות האילן הוא אומר בורא
פרי העץ חוץ מן היין שעל היין הוא אומר בורא פרי
הגפן ועל פירות הארץ הוא אומר בורא פרי האדמה חוץ מן הפת
שעל הפת הוא אומר המוציא לחם מן הארץ ועל הירקות הוא אומר
בורא פרי האדמה רבי יהודה אומר בורא מיני דשאים : גמ' מנא
ה"מ דתנו רבנן קדש הלולים לה' מלמד שטעונים ברכה לפניהם
ולאחריהם מכאן אמר ר"ע אסור לאדם שיטעום כלום קודם שיברך

ת"ר אסור לו לאדם שיהנה מן העוה"ז בלא ברכה וכל הנהנה מן
העוה"ז בלא ברכה מעל מאי תקנתיה ילך אצל חכם ילך אצל חכם
מאי עביד ליה הא עביד ליה איסורא אלא אמר רבא ילך אצל חכם
מעיקרא וילמדנו ברכות כדי שלא יבא לידי מעילה אמר רב יהודה
אמר שמואל כל הנהנה מן העוה"ז בלא ברכה כאילו נהנה מקדשי
שמים שנא' לה' הארץ ומלואה ר' לוי רמי כתיב לה' הארץ
ומלואה וכתיב השמים שמים לה' והארץ נתן לבני אדם לא קשיא
כאן קודם ברכה כאן לאחר ברכה א"ר חנינא בר פפא כל הנהנה
מן העוה"ז בלא ברכה כאילו גוזל להקב"ה וכנסת ישראל שנא'
גוזל אביו ואמו ואומר אין פשע חבר הוא לאיש משחית ואין אביו
אלא הקב"ה שנא' הלא הוא אביך קנך ואין אמו אלא כנסת ישראל
שנא' שמע בני מוסר אביך ואל תטוש תורת אמך מאי חבר הוא
לאיש משחית א"ר חנינא בר פפא חבר הוא לירבעם בן נבט
שהשחית את ישראל לאביהם שבשמים : ר' חנינא בר פפא רמי
כתיב ולקחתי דגני בעתו וגו' וכתיב ואספת דגנך וגו' ל"ק כאן בזמן
שישראל עושין רצונו של מקום כאן בזמן שאין ישראל עושין
רצונו של מקום ת"ר ואספת דגנך מה ת"ל לפי שנא' לא ימוש ספר
התורה הזה מפיך יכול דברים ככתבן ת"ל ואספת דגנך הנהג כהן
מנהג דרך ארץ דברי ר' ישמעאל ר"ש בן יוחי אומר אפשר אדם
חורש בשעת חרישה וזורע בשעת זריעה וקוצר בשעת קצירה ודש
בשעת דישה וזורה בשעת הרוח תורה מה תהא עליה אלא בזמן

שישראל עושין רצונו של מקום מלאכתן נעשית ע"י אחרים שנא'
ועמדו זרים ורעו צאנכם וגו' ובזמן שאין ישראל עושין רצונו של
מקום מלאכתן נעשית ע"י עצמן שנא' ואספת דגנך ולא עוד אלא
שמלאכת אחרים נעשית על ידן שנא' ועבדת את אויביך וגו' אמר
אביי הרבה עשו כרבי ישמעאל ועלתה בידן כר' שמעון בן יוחי ולא
עלתה בידן א"ל רבא לרבנן במטותא מינייכו ביומי ניסן וכיומי
תשרי לא תתחזו קמאי כי היכי דלא תטרדו במזונייכו כולא שתא :
אמר רבה בר בר חנה א"ר יוחנן משום רבי יהודה בר' אלעאי בא
וראה שלא כדורות הראשונים דורות האחרונים דורות הראשונים
עשו תורתן קבע ומלאכתן עראי זו וזו נתקיימה בידן דורות
האחרונים שעשו מלאכתן קבע ותורתן עראי זו וזו לא נתקיימה
בידן

nce more, you must be struck by the strange intrusion of whether we should spend all our time studying Torah. From our point of view, it simply is *not* a natural problem. But the person who put together this discussion saw the question as a routine turning.

The connection is formed by the reference to *gathering in grain*. The same verse of Scripture occurs in the two sequential discussions. Therefore, having brought up the subject of gathering grain, we are "naturally" going to talk about that subject.

The Talmud is concerned with a life of holiness, but we live in a world uninterested in what is holy.

The Talmud wants to talk about serving God, but people we know rarely think about such matters.

The Talmud literally believes everything that Scripture says. That is the first and most important truth you have learned in this book.

Scripture says if you serve God, you will have blessings, and if you do not serve God, you will have misfortune. And the rabbis of the Talmud believe that you serve God by studying Torah.

Our context, we remember, is how we say blessings for natural benefits. The reason, we recall, is that we say a blessing because the world belongs to God. Only when we say a blessing do we have a right to take what belongs to God and make it our own. And is not learning Torah a way to gain the right to make what is in the world our own?

If this is your worldly perspective, then it is natural to ask whether it is better both to work and to study Torah or only to study Torah. To the Talmudic rabbis who were devoted to Torah study this was a real and urgent question. For they also had to make a living for themselves and their families. In time to come, if your studies succeed, it should also become an issue for you.

The issue is our enjoyment of worldly benefits and the way in which we gain that right. What could be a more natural and obvious question than how to live the good life in the good world that God made for us? And since, for the rabbis, the good life is one of studying Torah, what could be more routine than to weigh the good life against the life of making a living.

A paradox exists. The world belongs to God, but we must work to gain the benefits that should come freely if we serve God. This is what troubles both Ishmael and Simeon b. Yohai according to the later Amoraim. Ishmael takes a reasonable position, but it is not logical within the Talmudic system. Simeon takes an unreasonable position, but within the system it makes good sense. When we first saw what they had to say, it seemed just the opposite. But now we turn matters around.

Simeon believes that God owns the world. He knows that if we do what the Torah requires, then we shall enjoy without struggle benefits of the world. So why should we not devote our lives to the study of Torah, so that God will bless us with what, after all, belongs to God? In the system we have laid out—as that system is revealed in the *Shema*, in the words of the prophets, and in the teachings of the rabbis themselves—Simeon's position is completely sensible.

Ishmael has one foot in and one foot outside the system. True, he is more practical. True, he deals with the world as it is, not with the world as the Torah describes it. True, many have followed his way and have lived good lives. But Simeon must object, "Is this really the good life?"

To see whether or not we have a single unit, we have to find the meanings of the individual components. Only then are we able to tell whether each unit is connected to the one before and leads directly to the one that follows.

I think that we have a natural and orderly presentation of ideas. But these are matters of taste and judgment. You have every right to form your own opinion once you have read the text with care and thought about what it says.

Once more we must ask whether the Talmud did a good job explaining the Mishnah-passage.

It has not done so in the passages we have considered. However, in some of the materials I did not present to you the Talmud makes important points about the Mishnah.

But we have a right to ask, "Has the Talmud said important things about the Mishnah? Has it made the Mishnah more important?"

I think the answer must be, Yes. For the Talmud has taken what is a routine matter—mumbling this blessing or that blessing—and shown us what is deep and important about it.

The Talmud has said something striking about deeds that we perform. It has explained that these deeds bear profound meanings for us, for our view of who we are, and for our understanding of our relationship to the world and to God.

So when the Talmud speaks about deeds, it talks of faith, of matters of belief. What is its message?

Nothing is to be taken for granted because everything is granted by God. We do not own the world by right. God who made the world owns it: "The earth is the Lord's, and the fulness thereof." Yet we are here and have needs, and God fills those needs. We should not act as if we own what is a gift, what is in our hands for only a little while.

We have to revere the natural world and treat with respect those things that God has made.

We have to be grateful for the gifts of nature and treat with high regard and thankfulness what is given to us.

And yet, how great are we, for whom all these things have been done! Who are we to deserve it all? And why is it all coming to us? The answers to these questions will be coming in the next unit of the Talmud. We really do not deserve all that we get. God gives us what we do not deserve and have not earned.

120

The important point is that when we speak about things we are supposed to do—about *halakhah*—we find we cannot be silent about things we are supposed to believe—about *aggadah*. When the Mishnah tells us about deeds, the Talmud tells us about beliefs. In Part Five, we shall see the opposite. When the Mishnah tells us about beliefs, the Talmud speaks about deeds: prayers we say at this time, prayers we say at that time. But the deeds are the deeds of faith, and the faith is a faith of deeds. There is no Mishnah without Talmud, there is no *halakhah* without *aggadah,* and there is no *aggadah* without *halakhah.*

We conclude by asking one more time: "What are the choices among which the person who made up our Talmud has made a selection? What are the things that might have been mentioned?

Only when we realize what might have been shall we truly understand what is. That applies to the Talmud. It also applies to the world in which we live.

WHAT IS THE TALMUD?

There can be only one answer to that question on the basis of the Talmud we have just learned. It is: the Talmud is a sustained and demanding essay about our religious life.

It takes off from the Mishnah, but it flies in the skies of its own discovery.

When the Mishnah tells us *what* to do, the Talmud asks *why* we should do it.

And the Talmud's answer explores the deep questions, Who are we? Where are we? What do we owe to God? What do we owe to one another? The Talmud's conception of the Mishnah is that these questions have yet to be answered. That means the Talmud is a criticism of the Mishnah.

The Talmud says what the Mishnah has not said. It not only serves to explain the Mishnah's language and ideas. It not only wants to tell us about the sources of the Mishnah's rules. It has an independent view of the Mishnah. It is not only the servant of the Mishnah. It is also the critic of the Mishnah.

Its response to a given Mishnah-passage tells us what the Talmud does not find in the Mishnah at all, as well as what the Talmud finds unclear or incomplete in the Mishnah. What the Talmud asks about "how we say blessings" is why we say blessings at all. And that means that the Talmud is dissatisfied with the Mishnah.

The Talmud is a long and serious criticism of the Mishnah. It judges what the Mishnah says, and it offers an opinion on what the Mishnah does not say.

That is not to suggest that the Talmud rejects the Mishnah. The Talmud respects the Mishnah. But the Talmud, in some measure, is independent of the Mishnah. It goes its own way. It asks its own questions. It raises its own issues for analysis.

That is why when the Mishnah speaks of blessing fruit, vegetables, wine, and bread, the Talmud talks of Torah and its study.

Here the Talmud has done much more than explain the implications of Mishnah's rule. No one can claim that Mishnah speaks of Torah when it mentions apples and loaves of bread. Here the Talmud has also done more than go beyond the frontiers laid out by the Mishnah's treatment of a law. The Talmud gives us more than important new ideas about that same law that Mishnah lays forth in some other aspect or detail.

The Talmud now shows us what it can do when it leaves the Mishnah behind entirely and proposes to talk about its own topics and interests. And what it can and does do is striking. The Mishnah is left behind in order to bring forward Mishnah's deepest meaning.

PART FIVE

The Talmud Speaks to Us about Beliefs and Deeds

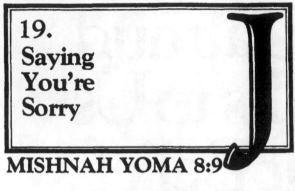

19. Saying You're Sorry

MISHNAH YOMA 8:9

Just as the law of the Talmud expresses beliefs we hold about what it means to be a human being and what we must do to live a holy life, so beliefs we hold create Talmudic law. That is, *halakhah* makes concrete what *aggadah* says in general terms. *Halakhah* brings down to everyday life what *aggadah* leaves up in heaven.

And the opposite is also true. If we hold a belief, which is expressed through *aggadah*, then *halakhah* comes into being to give form and concreteness to that belief. There cannot be a belief without an action to express that belief. We are what we do. Our beliefs *define* what we are, and our deeds *express* what we are.

To see how beliefs make laws necessary, we turn to a Mishnah-passage about the Day of Atonement and sin. In a religious system such as ours, in which there are so many things we are supposed to do or supposed not to do, it is inevitable that we shall do something wrong. We are human. It is not natural for us to keep all the laws. Some of the ritual ones may be inconvenient.

Much more important: *some of the rules about right action to our fellow human beings conflict with our deep needs to be selfish and to hurt other people.* So we do sin, and when we do, it is more commonly against other people than it is against God.

We know that the Day of Atonement brings forgiveness and reconciliation between us and God. But what about forgiveness for what we have done against other people? For that purpose, we have to rely upon our own efforts. The Day of Atonement will not do for us what we do not do for ourselves.

The Mishnah and the Talmud are able to work out general rules to tell us what to do in ordinary circumstances. This is hardly as easy as it sounds. Since the Mishnah and the Talmud go back for nearly two thousand years, it is amazing that they are still interesting to us. We live in a completely different age and in a totally different world. How is it possible for us to *want* to hear what the Mishnah and the Talmud have to tell us about our relationships with other people?

The reason is in two parts.

First, because human relationships do remain constant. There are just so many things people can do to and for each other, bad things and good things.

Second, because the Mishnah and the Talmud, for their part, are careful to avoid talking about things in a too concrete and specific way. If they are too specific, people will eventually no longer listen to what they have to say.

The Mishnah, as we shall see, speaks about fundamental and enduring truths, things that last from age to age and go on from place to place. It talks about sin and saying you're sorry ("repentance"), about relying upon the Day of Atonement to do what we can and should do for ourselves. The Mishnah speaks of winning the friendship of people whom we have offended. It is surely relevant to us. We have friends whom we have offended. It certainly speaks to our world and about our problems.

It is no accident. The conception of the Mishnah and the Talmud is that we can discover rules that will apply everywhere and to all the Jewish people. That is why the Mishnah and the Talmud claim to be Torah. They speak eternal truths—which God reveals and which we accept as Torah—even though they were written down long after Moses received the Torah at Mount Sinai. The power of Mishnah and Talmud lies in their ability to talk to us.

But you are the one who gives the Mishnah and the Talmud their power and influence.

Once more we want to know, therefore, how the Mishnah and the accompanying Talmud arrange things that Jews already say and do. We want to examine, in particular, the Talmud's mode of thinking and analyzing practices. Finally, we hope to see what we may learn from the Talmud about things with which we already are familiar.

As you will see, the Mishnah before us is a set of four sentences, each separate and distinct from the others.

| 1 | He who says | הָאוֹמֵר: |
| | I shall sin and repent, sin and repent | אֶחֱטָא וְאָשׁוּב, אֶחֱטָא וְאָשׁוּב - |

they do not give him sufficient power to make repentance

אֵין מַסְפִּיקִין בְּיָדוֹ לַעֲשׂוֹת תְּשׁוּבָה;

[He who says], I shall sin, and the Day of Atonement will atone

אֶחֱטָא, וְיוֹם הַכִּפּוּרִים מְכַפֵּר ־

the Day of Atonement does not atone

אֵין יוֹם הַכִּפּוּרִים מְכַפֵּר.

2 Sins that are between man and the Omnipresent the Day of Atonement atones for.

עֲבֵרוֹת שֶׁבֵּין אָדָם לַמָּקוֹם ־
יוֹם הַכִּפּוּרִים מְכַפֵּר;

Sins that are between man and his fellow

עֲבֵרוֹת שֶׁבֵּין אָדָם לַחֲבֵרוֹ ־

the Day of Atonement does not atone for,

אֵין יוֹם הַכִּפּוּרִים מְכַפֵּר,

until one will win the good will of his fellow [once more].

עַד שֶׁיְּרַצֶּה אֶת חֲבֵרוֹ.

3 This is what Rabbi Eleazar ben Azariah expounded:

אֶת זוֹ דָּרַשׁ רַבִּי אֶלְעָזָר בֶּן עֲזַרְיָה:

From all your sins shall you be clean before the Lord (Lev. 16:3)

„מִכֹּל חַטֹּאתֵיכֶם לִפְנֵי יְיָ תִּטְהָרוּ";

Sins that are between man and the Omnipresent

עֲבֵרוֹת שֶׁבֵּין אָדָם לַמָּקוֹם ־

the Day of Atonement atones for.

יוֹם הַכִּפּוּרִים מְכַפֵּר.

Sins that are between man and his fellow

עֲבֵרוֹת שֶׁבֵּין אָדָם לַחֲבֵרוֹ ־

the Day of Atonement does not atone for

אֵין יוֹם הַכִּפּוּרִים מְכַפֵּר,

until one will win the good will of his fellow.

עַד שֶׁיְּרַצֶּה אֶת חֲבֵרוֹ.

4 Said Rabbi Aqiva
   Happy are you, Oh Israel!
   Before whom are you purified?
   Who purifies you?
   Your father who is in heaven.
   As it is said, And I will
   sprinkle clean water on you
   and you will be clean
   (Ezekiel 36:25).
   And it says, "The hope of
   Israel is the Lord (Jeremiah
   17:13)."
   Just as the immersion-pool
   cleans the unclean people,
   So the Holy One blessed be he
   cleans Israel.

אָמַר רַבִּי עֲקִיבָא:

אַשְׁרֵיכֶם יִשְׂרָאֵל!

לִפְנֵי מִי אַתֶּם מִטַּהֲרִין?

מִי מְטַהֵר אֶתְכֶם?

אֲבִיכֶם שֶׁבַּשָּׁמַיִם,

שֶׁנֶּאֱמַר: „וְזָרַקְתִּי עֲלֵיכֶם

מַיִם טְהוֹרִים וּטְהַרְתֶּם";

וְאוֹמֵר: „מִקְוֵה יִשְׂרָאֵל ה'";

מַה הַמִּקְוֶה מְטַהֵר אֶת הַטְּמֵאִים,

אַף הַקָּדוֹשׁ בָּרוּךְ הוּא מְטַהֵר

אֶת יִשְׂרָאֵל.

Vocabulary

he who says	הָאוֹמֵר	he appeases	יְרַצֶּה
I will sin	אֶחֱטָא	expound	דָּרַשׁ
I will repent	אָשׁוּב	your sins	חַטֹּאתֵיכֶם
there is no	אֵין	before	לִפְנֵי
opportunity	מַסְפִּיקִין	you will be clean	תִּטְהָרוּ
for him	בְּיָדוֹ	you are happy	אַשְׁרֵיכֶם
to do	לַעֲשׂוֹת	your father	אֲבִיכֶם
repentance	תְּשׁוּבָה	in heaven	בַּשָּׁמַיִם
Yom Kippur	יוֹם הַכִּפּוּרִים	as it is written	שֶׁנֶּאֱמַר
effect atonement	מְכַפֵּר	I will sprinkle	זָרַקְתִּי
transgressions	עֲבֵרוֹת	on you	עֲלֵיכֶם
between	בֵּין	water	מַיִם
man	אָדָם	hope	מִקְוֶה
The Omnipresent	הַמָּקוֹם	the immersion-pool	הַמִּקְוֶה
his fellow	חֲבֵרוֹ	the unclean	הַטְּמֵאִים
until	עַד		

The Mishnah-passage repeats its idea four times, each time in a somewhat different way. The main point is that the Day of Atonement will do us no good if we do not do our share of the work of repentance. We must say that we're sorry for what we have done wrong. The first point is that we cannot sin and take for granted that the Day of Atonement will make up for us. There is nothing magical, nothing that works without regard to what we do and believe in our hearts. The second point is that the Day of Atonement serves only to atone for those sins that we have done against God. But sins that we have done against other people must be atoned for by going to the person whom we have injured and seeking forgiveness.

Our Mishnah is going to demand some amplification here. What sort of "mission" to the one whom we have hurt is required? What if the person will not grant us forgiveness? These are questions of belief, but they are going to demand statements of behavior—rules on what we are expected to do.

The third and the fourth points say what the first two points already have said. Eleazar b. Azariah's lesson is precisely what No. 2 already has told us. The Day of Atonement will do us good only if we first seek forgiveness of the one we have injured.

Before we proceed to the Talmud, let us see whether we are able to list some of the questions we shall want the Talmud to answer.

First, we shall want to know the source of the Mishnah-passage's rule. That source, we need hardly note, is Scripture. So we shall ask, "What is the source of this rule about seeking forgiveness from our friend?"

We shall ask the Talmud to tell us whether we must persist, if the friend will not forgive, and if so, to what extent.

What if the person whom we have hurt moves away, or dies, before we have a chance to gain forgiveness? What do we do then?

These are some of the things we shall not expect the Talmud to tell us, when the Talmud comes before us in its role as an explanation for the Mishnah. What the Talmud will tell us when it proceeds to expand and explain its explanation we can now hardly predict.

20. Explaining the Mishnah

By this time in your learning of Talmud, you surely can predict that the first thing the Talmud will want to know about this Mishnah-passage is the source of this law. Sometimes the question is asked directly. Other times, the question is answered without being asked. In the first Talmud-selection, we find the answer without the question. Naturally, the answer is that we learn the rule in Scripture.

This time the relevant book of the Bible is Proverbs, and we shall observe that Proverbs says almost exactly what the Mishnah says. But it says the same thing in a different circumstance and for a different purpose. So the contribution of the Amora Isaac is to see the relevance of what Scripture says to what Mishnah wants us to do. This we shall see in A-J.

We already know to expect that when we have a statement of an ideal of how we should behave, the Talmud will turn that statement into rules about things we must actually do. We therefore shall not be surprised to find that an important explanation of our Mishnah-passage will be a concrete instruction on precisely how to make friends with someone we have offended. The rule will be spun out of a relevant verse of Scripture since, you remember, the Amoraim do not regard Mishnah as an adequate and complete source of truth. They insist on turning, also and especially, to the written Torah, to the Scriptures. Two Amoraim, Hisda (K-O) and Yose b. R. Hanina (P-Z), supply us with rules based upon verses of the Scripture.

A. Said R. Isaac,	אָמַר ר׳ יִצְחָק,
B. Whoever offends his fellow,	כָּל הַמַּקְנִיט אֶת חֲבֵירוֹ,
C. even [merely] through words,	אֲפִילוּ בִּדְבָרִים,
D. has to make peace with him,	צָרִיךְ לְפַיְּיסוֹ,
E. since it is said,	שֶׁנֶּאֱמַר,

F. My son, if you have become a surety for your neighbor, if you have struck your hands for a stranger, you are snared by the words of your mouth. Do this now, my son, and deliver yourself, since you have come into the hand of your neighbor. Go, humble yourself, and urge your neighbor (Prov. 6:1-3).

G. If you are wealthy

H. open the palm of your hand to him.

I. And if not

J. send many friends to him.

K. Said R. Hisda,

L. And he needs to make peace with him through three groups of three people,

M. since it is said,

N. He comes before men and says,

O. I have sinned, and I have perverted that which was right, and it did me no profit (Job 33:27).

P. Said R. Yosé b. R. Hanina,

Q. Whoever seeks pardon of his fellow

R. should not seek it from him more than three times,

S. since it is said, Forgive, I pray you now, and now we pray you (Gen. 50:17).

בְּנִי אִם
עָרַבְתָּ לְרֵעֶךָ,
תָּקַעְתָּ לַזָּר כַּפֶּיךָ,
נוֹקַשְׁתָּ
בְאִמְרֵי פִיךָ.
עֲשֵׂה זֹאת אֵפוֹא בְּנִי
וְהִנָּצֵל, כִּי בָאתָ
בְכַף רֵעֶךָ. לֵךְ הִתְרַפֵּס
וּרְהַב רֵעֶיךָ.

אִם מָמוֹן יֵשׁ בְּיָדְךָ
הַתֵּר לוֹ פִּסַּת יָד,
וְאִם לָאו,
הַרְבֵּה עָלָיו רֵיעִים.
אָמַר רַב חִסְדָּא,
וְצָרִיךְ לְפַיְּיסוֹ
בְּשָׁלֹשׁ שׁוּרוֹת
שֶׁל שְׁלֹשָׁה בְּנֵי אָדָם,
שֶׁנֶּאֱמַר,
יָשׁוֹר עַל אֲנָשִׁים וַיֹּאמֶר

חָטָאתִי,
וְיָשָׁר הֶעֱוֵיתִי,
וְלֹא שָׁוָה לִי.

(וְאָמַר) ר׳ יוֹסֵי בַּר חֲנִינָא,
כָּל הַמְבַקֵּשׁ מָטוּ
מֵחֲבֵירוֹ,
אַל יְבַקֵּשׁ מִמֶּנּוּ
יוֹתֵר מִשָּׁלֹשׁ פְּעָמִים,
שֶׁנֶּאֱמַר, אָנָּא שָׂא נָא ...
וְעַתָּה שָׂא נָא.

130

T. But if he dies,   וְאִם מֵת,

U. one brings ten men,   מֵבִיא עֲשָׂרָה בְּנֵי אָדָם

V. and sets them up at his grave,   וּמַעֲמִידָן עַל קִבְרוֹ,

W. and says,   וְאוֹמֵר,

Y. "I have sinned against the Lord, the God of Israel,   חָטָאתִי לה׳ אֱלֹהֵי יִשְׂרָאֵל

Z. "and against Mr. So and So, whom I have injured."   וְלִפְלוֹנִי שֶׁחָבַלְתִּי בּוֹ.

Vocabulary

one who offends	הַמַּקְנִיט	it did me no profit	לֹא שָׁוָה לִי
even	אֲפִילוּ	one who seeks	הַמְבַקֵּשׁ
to make peace	לְפַיֵּיס	pardon	מָטוּ
wealth	מָמוֹן	times	פְּעָמִים
friends	רֵיעִים	ten	עֲשָׂרָה
groups	שׁוּרוֹת	sets them up	מַעֲמִידָן
people	בְּנֵי אָדָם	grave	קֶבֶר
I have sinned	חָטָאתִי	I have injured	חָבַלְתִּי
I have perverted what is right	יָשָׁר הֶעֱוֵיתִי		

saac's rule is not quite the same as Mishnah's, since the Mishnah-passage speaks of the setting of the Day of Atonement. So why has the Talmudic editor introduced this rule at just this point? For the obvious reason that the Mishnah-passage speaks about harm done by a person to another person. It says that the Day of Atonement does not atone in such a case. You must apologize and win the other person's forgiveness. So Isaac's

131

saying (A-J) is quite appropriate for this setting, even though it is not exactly to the point of the Mishnah-passage. In fact, what he says is rather straight-forward, even self-evident. If you offend your fellow, even by something you have said, you have to make peace.

The proof-text then becomes the main element. Proverbs 6:1-3 contains precisely the advice that Isaac wants to give. If someone has a claim of money against you, pay him off. If it is some other sort of complaint, send many friends to him: "Urge your neighbor."

Hisda's point is equally clear. The work of making friends should not go on indefinitely. You try your best. But if the other person cannot be pacified, then let it be. Three times, with three people each time, would be ample. You notice that the verse in Job contains three clauses. The person says, "I have sinned," and then, "I have perverted," and finally, "and it did me no profit." So we find three little "confessions," a fair indication of what is required of you as well.

Yose b. R. Hanina then draws out the implications of Hisda's saying. You do it three times—and no more than three times. This is derived not from what Hisda has said but from yet another verse of Scripture, cited at S. Here, too, we see a group of three clauses and each represents a request for pardon and forgiveness.

Finally we have the rule to cover the special case of someone's dying before we can make up. The Talmud's answer is to go to the grave and to state there the confession of what one has done, together with a prayer for forgiveness. It is the best you can do. You should not misunderstand the point of going to the grave. It is to help the person who seeks forgiveness to locate and focus upon the one who has been injured. Going to the grave is for the sake of the one who is alive, not for the sake of the one whose bones are deposited in the ground.

It is time to ask whether—if you were commenting on and explaining this Mishnah-passage—you would add to what the Talmud contributes. Can you make up a Talmud to go along with the one given to us by the Amoraim of Babylonia of the third, fourth, and fifth centuries of the Common Era? This is a good opportunity since the teachings of the Amoraim are expressed fairly simply and they address an issue that you know well. How would you make up—continue—the Talmud?

You might add some stories of specific incidents you have witnessed such as occasions on which someone you know has tried to make friends with a person he or she has made angry or offended. Or you might amplify Yose's case about someone who dies. You might add that if someone moves away, you write letters or make phone calls.

The concluding unit of our Talmudic passage shows us how the person who put the Talmud together added to these rather straight-forward rules and made the Talmudic passage more concrete. This was done by adding a series of three stories about what happened to great rabbis of the Talmudic age.

II. A. R. Jeremiah had
something against R. Abba.
      ר׳ יִרְמְיָה הֲוָה לֵיה מִילְתָא
      לר׳ אַבָּא בַּהֲדֵיה

B. He went and sat down at
the door of R. Abba.
      אֲזַל אֵיתִיב אַדַּשָׁא
      דר׳ אַבָּא.

C. As the maid was throwing
out water,
      בַּהֲדֵי דְשַׁדְיָא אַמְתֵיה
      מַיָּא,

D. a few drops of water
touched his head.
      מְטָא זַרְזִיסֵי דְמַיָּא
      אַרֵישָׁא.

E. He said, They have made
me into a dung-heap.
      אֲמַר עֲשָׂאוּנִי
      כָּאַשְׁפָּה.

F. He cited the following verse
about himself:
      קָרָא אַנַּפְשֵׁיה:

G. He raises up the poor out of
the dust (I Samuel 2:8).
      מֵאַשְׁפּוֹת יָרִים אֶבְיוֹן.

H. R. Abba heard.
      שָׁמַע ר׳ אַבָּא

I. And he came to him.
      וּנְפַק לְאַפֵּיה.

J. He said to him,
      אֲמַר לֵיה,

K. Now I must make peace
with you.
      הַשְׁתָּא צְרִיכְנָא לְמֵיפַק אֲדַעְתָּךְ

L. For it is written,
      דִּכְתִיב,

M. Go, humble yourself and
urge your neighbor (Prov.
6:3).
      לֵךְ הִתְרַפֵּס וּרְהַב
      רֵעֶיךָ.

Vocabulary

had	הֲוָה	drops	זַרְזִיפֵי
something	מִילְתָא	they have made me	עֲשָׂאוּנִי
he went	אֲזַל	dung-heap	אַשְׁפָּה
he sat	אֵיתִיב	he came out	נָפֵיק
door	דַּשָּׁא	to him	לְאַפֵּיה
as	בַּהֲדֵי	now	הַשְׁתָּא
throwing	שַׁדְיָא	I must	צְרִיכְנָא
his maid	אַמְתֵיה	make peace with you	לְמֵיפַק אַרְעָתָךְ
water	מַיָּא		
touched	מָטָא		

The story's purpose is to give the law life. The law takes on new and human meaning when we are told how a particular sage acted. That is why the editor of the Talmud placed this and two other stories alongside the Talmud's explanation and expansion of our Mishnah-passage. But the stories also have their own purposes. They make their own points. It is only later on that the person who put the Talmud together as we have it brought them before us and set them out as illustrations of the Talmud's explanation of the Mishnah-passage.

Jeremiah's behavior is interesting. Jeremiah had injured Abba. So Jeremiah went straight to the other party and sat down at his door. What was the importance of such a deed? It was to make sure that Abba knew that Jeremiah was aware something had gone wrong. Why? Because Jeremiah understood that the worst thing Abba could do is to bear a grudge. If you are angry and you express it, the ball is in the other person's court. You do not keep things in. You say what you think. If the other party wants to make amends, well and good. But you are not going to hate that other person.

The way to avoid hating him or her is to say what you think. Then why

134

be angry any longer? So Jeremiah went and sat down at Abba's door. It was a simple, silent, and eloquent gesture. Let Abba say what was on his mind.

What happened? The maid threw out some water, and Jeremiah got slightly wet. Just a few drops touched him. But to him this was too much. So he pitied himself. This is not so impressive. But it had a good result. Jeremiah quoted a verse from Scripture, with the notion that the verse spoke about Jeremiah in particular: "He raises up the poor out of the dust." Now Abba heard that Jeremiah was at his door. He came out and realized what was happening. Then he, too, found an appropriate verse in Scripture—that same verse with which we began our account, cited by Isaac to explain and support the teaching of the Mishnah-passage. So you can see that whatever really happened, the story is worked out to remind us of where we are, which is in the Talmudic discussion. This is artful, since in the story itself, the cited verse of Scripture plays an important role as well.

A. R. Zeira, when he had something against some one,	ר׳ זֵירָא כִּי הֲוָה לֵיה מִילְתָא בַּהֲדֵי אִינִישׁ
B. would go back and forth before him,	הֲוָה חָלֵיף וְתָנֵי לְקַמֵּיהּ
C. and make himself available to the other,	וּמַמְצִיא לֵיהּ,
D. so that the other would come out	כִּי הֵיכִי דְּנֵיתִי
E. and make peace with him.	וְנֵיפּוֹק לֵיהּ מִדַּעֲתֵיהּ.

against some one	בַּהֲדֵי אִינִישׁ
go back and forth	חָלֵיף וְתָנֵי
before him	לְקַמֵּיהּ
make himself available	מַמְצִיא
so that	כִּי הֵיכִי
come out	נֵיתִי

he story-teller reports something Zeira did under ordinary circumstances, a general rule of behavior, rather than a specific and concrete incident. When someone hurt Zeira, he would go to the other party and say nothing. He simply made himself available. The other person would then see him and do what had to be done. Why has the editor told this story at this point? For the obvious reason that Zeira is said here to have done in general what Jeremiah did in particular. So the story is not told at random or without purpose. It is part of a careful discussion of the notion that if you have a grievance, don't keep it in. Go to the other party. But you don't have to say a thing. All you have to do is remind the other party by your presence that there is some unfinished business.

The third story then proceeds to illustrate the same thing. But it makes another point as well.

A. Rab [Rab Abba] had something against a certain butcher.	רַב הֲוָה לֵיהּ מִילְתָא בַּהֲדֵי הַהוּא טַבָּחָא;
B. He [the butcher] did not come to him [Rab].	לָא אָתָא לְקַמֵיהּ.
C. On the eve of the Day of Atonement, he [Rab] said, I shall go to make peace with him.	בְּמַעֲלֵי יוֹמָא דְכִפּוּרֵי אָמַר אִיהוּ אֵיזֵיל אֲנָא לְפִיּוּסֵי לֵיהּ.
D. R. Huna met him.	פְּגַע בֵּיהּ רַב הוּנָא.
E. He said to him, Where is the master going?	אָמַר לֵיהּ לְהֵיכָא קָא אָזֵיל מַר,
F. He said to him, "To make peace with so-and-so."	אָמַר לֵיהּ לְפִיּוּסֵי לִפְלַנְיָא.
G. He said, "Abba is going to kill someone."	אָמַר אָזֵיל אַבָּא לְמִיקְטַל נַפְשָׁא.

H. He [Rab] went and stood before him.

אֲזַל וְקָם עִילָוֵיה.

I. He [the butcher] was sitting and chopping an [animal's] head.

הֲוָה יָתֵיב וְקָא סָלֵי רֵישָׁא.

J. He [the butcher] raised his eyes and saw him.

דַּלֵי עֵינֵיה וְחַזְיֵיה,

K. He said to him, "You are Abba! Get out. I have nothing to do with you."

אֲמַר לֵיה אַבָּא אַתְ זִיל, לֵית לִי מִילְתָא בַּהֲדָךְ.

L. While he was chopping the head,

בַּהֲדֵי דְקָא סָלֵי רֵישָׁא

M. a bone flew off,

אִישְׁתַּמֵיט גַּרְמָא

N. and stuck his throat,

וּמְחַיֵיה בְּקוֹעֵיה,

O. and killed him.

וְקַטְלֵיה.

Vocabulary

butcher	טַבְּחָא	chopping	סָלֵי
the eve of the Day of Atonement	מַעֲלֵי יוֹמָא דְכִפּוּרֵי	head	רֵישָׁא
		he raised	דַּלֵי
this one	אִיהוּ	his eyes	עֵינֵיה
I shall go	אֵיזִיל אֲנָא	saw him	חַזְיֵיה
to make peace with him	לְפַיוּסֵי לֵיה	get out	זִיל
		I have nothing	לֵית לִי
where?	לְהֵיכָא	to do with you	מִילְתָא בַּהֲדָךְ
going	אָזֵיל	while	בַּהֲדֵי
the master	מַר	he was chopping	קָא סָלֵי
so-and-so	לִפְלַנְיָא	flew off	אִישְׁתַּמֵיט
to kill	לְמִיקְטַל	a bone	גַּרְמָא
someone	נַפְשָׁא	stuck	מְחַיֵיה
before him	עִילָוֵיה	his throat	קוֹעֵיה
sitting	יָתֵיב	killed him	קַטְלֵיה

he story about Rab goes over the same ground as the stories we already have heard. That is, you have to make yourself available to the party against whom you have a grievance. You don't sit on your high horse. You go to the other person. That is what Rab did.

But our opening Talmudic passage has made a second point. If the editor is not to lose that other point, we have to be reminded of it. What if the other party will not then seek to reconcile with you? This is not quite the point of Isaac and Hisda and Yose, which is that you make an effort to appease the other party. But the important and new idea is precisely this: What happens if you go to the other party, and that person will not atone for the harm he or she has done to you? What do you do then? So the new and final notion of this carefully constructed set completes the whole. Review the points:

1. If you offend your friend, you have to try to appease him or her (Isaac).

2. You send three groups of people, in succession (Hisda).

3. If the friend will not be appeased, you owe no more (Yose b. Hanina).

4. If your friend has a grievance *against you,* you make yourself available (Jeremiah, thus illustrating the general position of Isaac and Hisda).

5. If you have a grievance *against your friend,* you make yourself available (Zeira).

6. If you have a grievance against your friend, you make yourself available. But if the friend will not then try to make amends, that is not your problem.

In No. 6 we conclude the line of thought begun by Isaac and Hisda.

Now the story about Rab is rather curious. It invokes something we have not seen often in our passages of the Talmud—supernatural power. When Rab is mistreated by the man, the man "accidentally" dies. The story-teller does not have to tell us that it is not an accident, but he does so when he has Huna make his prophetic comment. The story-teller wants us to know that the butcher's accidental death is not accidental. So we are warned in advance, through Huna's baleful comment, that Rab, in all innocence, is protected by Heaven.

Rab behaved correctly. Indeed, the story about Rab is the first point in this sequence that reminds us where we began, the Day of Atonement. Until this story, the subject has never been mentioned! So it is the Day of Atonement. In conformity with the Mishnah's teaching, we should have expected the butcher to come to Rab, as Jeremiah did. But the butcher did not come. So, like Zeira, Rab makes himself available to the butcher. Huna intervenes early to warn us of the story's real meaning. Then, the story resumes (H). If we did not have D-G, the story would flow smoothly. But it also would not make its point.

Rab goes to the butcher and stands up before him—a respectful gesture indeed, since it is Rab who has the complaint against the butcher. I underlines Rab's strange and deliberate behavior. It reminds us that the butcher remains sitting. And, lest we miss the point and think the butcher did stand up, we are told that he merely raised his eyes and saw Rab (J). The butcher remained seated in the presence of one of the great sages of the time. It is a sage, moreover, whom the butcher offended, and it is the eve of the Day of Atonement. All the elements are present for some smashing conclusion. And it is not long in coming. The butcher speaks his own death-sentence in K. "You are Abba—get out!" The world is on its head. The person who is injured is injured again. And all of this is done with great brutality—the butcher continues to chop the animal head (L). The rest follows.

The butcher chops the head—the symbol of death—and a bone flies off and sticks in the butcher's throat. He is injured by his own actions, and the bone stabs him in the organ that he has used to injure and offend Rab. The butcher died because he killed himself. The irony of Huna's saying now is clear. Abba (that is, Rab) killed no one. The butcher did not really kill himself. It was an accident. But Huna has already told us the meaning of the accident.

Now why has the one who put the Talmud together told this story here? We notice that there are three *halakhic* sayings, Isaac's, Hisda's, and Yose b. R. Hanina's. Then we have three stories that illustrate *halakhah*, Abba-Jeremiah, Zeira, and Rab. And the climax is surely here. We recall where we started—the Day of Atonement, appeasing your friend.

We end at precisely the unanswered question: What happens if you do not appease your friend, whom you have injured, by the eve of the Day of Atonement?

True, it is an extreme and unusual case. What happens with Rab here happens because, after all, Rab is a holy man and a great sage of Torah. Still, the story in its own context is not making the point that Rab is a holy man and that we should not be mean to rabbis. It makes the point that Rab was the injured party and he went to the one who had hurt him (as Zeira did) in order to give the other party a chance to deal with his complaint (as Abba did). And this he did on the eve of the Day of Atonement just as the Mishnah says we must do. So the concluding story, which brings us back to the Mishnah-passage, also has a powerful effect in answering the question the Mishnah has left open:

What happens if you do not do what the Mishnah says?

The answer is, God oversees all things. God seals our judgment on the Day of Atonement. If, therefore, on the eve of the Day of Atonement, we do not do what is expected of us, there will be serious results.

This artful construction, therefore, has never lost sight of the Mishnah-passage it is meant to explain even though, as we ourselves have seen, it is sometimes difficult to keep our eyes on our starting point. In the end, we can rely on the one who put things together. We never are let down.

You will recall that once before we asked ourselves, "Is the Talmud carefully constructed, or is it just one interesting saying or story after another?" We once more observe that the Talmud, as exemplified by this passage, is put together with amazing care. We see there is close attention to form and formality. Three of one thing, then a matching triplet: three teachings, three stories. We see that acute care is paid to the substance as each saying, then each story, carries forward what has been set in the preceding one. And, at the end, we see a remarkable climax—the invocation of God's role in making sense of the whole thing. And at the end, we return to the beginning. We show the relevance to the Mishnah-passage of all that the Talmud has said by way of explaining the Mishnah-passage.

21. Expanding the Explanation

The Talmud's next important passage goes on to fresh ideas. It deals with the *Confession*, the recital of sins that we say on the Day of Atonement. The Day of Atonement atones for our sins, so we must list those sins before God in order to seek forgiveness. The Talmud's discussion carries forward, in a general way, its treatment of our Mishnah-passage. The Mishnah-passage provides the theme of forgiveness of sins on the Day of Atonement. But the specific treatment of the theme is another matter.

The Talmud has two questions about the confession of sins. First, when are we supposed to confess our sins? Second, precisely what prayer do we say to confess our sins?

Before we proceed, let us look at the prayer that nowadays we say in the synagogue as the confession of sins on the Day of Atonement. It is known as the *Vidui*, or Confession, and appears in the *Mahzor*, the Prayerbook for the New Year and the Day of Atonement, as follows (in the translation of Rabbi Jules Harlow):

We abuse, we betray, we are cruel.
We destroy, we embitter, we falsify.
We gossip, we hate, we insult.
We jeer, we kill, we lie.
We mock, we neglect, we oppress.
We pervert, we quarrel, we rebel.
We steal, we transgress, we are unkind.
We are violent, we are wicked, we are xenophobic.
We yield to evil, we are zealots for bad causes.

We have ignored Your commandments and statutes, and it has not profited us. You are just, we have stumbled. You have acted faithfully, we have been unrighteous.

We have sinned, we have transgressed. Therefore we have not been saved. Endow us with the will to forsake evil; save us soon. Thus Your prophet Isaiah declared: "Let the wicked forsake his path, and the unrigh-

teous man his plottings. Let him return to the Lord, who will show him compassion. Let him return to our God, who will surely forgive him."

Our God and God of our fathers, forgive and pardon our sins on this Shabbot and on this Yom Kippur. Answer our prayers by removing our transgressions from Your sight. Subdue our impulse to evil; submit us to Your service, that we may return to You. Renew our will to observe Your precepts. Soften our hardened hearts so that we may love and revere You, as it is written in Your Torah: "And the Lord your God will soften your heart and the heart of your children, so that you will love the Lord your God with all your heart and with all your being that you may live."

You know our sins, whether deliberate or not, whether committed willingly or under compulsion, whether in public or in private. What are we? What is our piety? What is our righteousness, our attainment, our power, our might? What can we say Lord our God and God of our fathers? Compared to You, all the mighty are nothing, the famous are non-existent, the wise lack wisdom, the clever lack reason. For most of their actions are meaninglessness, the days of their lives emptiness. Man's superiority to the beast is an illusion. All life is a fleeting breath.

What can we say to You, what can we tell You? You know all things, secret and revealed.

You always forgive transgressions. Hear the cry of our prayers. Pass over the transgressions of a people who turn away from transgression. Blot out our sins from Your sight.

You know the mysteries of the universe, the secrets of everyone alive. You probe our innermost depths. You examine our thoughts and desires. Nothing escapes You, nothing is hidden from You.

May it therefore be Your will, Lord our God and God of our fathers, to forgive us all our sins, to pardon all our iniquities, to grant us atonement for all our transgressions.

We have sinned against You unwillingly and willingly.
And we have sinned against You by misusing our minds.
We have sinned against You by immoral sexual acts.
And we have sinned against you knowingly and deceitfully.
We have sinned against You by wronging others.
And we have sinned against You by supporting immorality.
We have sinned against You by deriding parents and teachers.

142

And we have sinned against You by using violence.
We have sinned against You by being foul-mouthed.
And we have sinned against You by not resisting the impulse to evil.

For all these sins, forgiving God, forgive us, pardon us, grant us atonement.

We have sinned against You by fraud and by falsehood.
And we have sinned against You by scoffing.
We have sinned against You by dishonesty in business.
And we have sinned against You by taking usurious interest.
We have sinned against You by idle chatter.
And we have sinned against You by haughtiness.
We have sinned against You by rejecting responsibility.
And we have sinned against You by plotting against others.
We have sinned against You by irreverence.
And we have sinned against You by rushing to do evil.
We have sinned against You by taking vain oaths.
And we have sinned against You by breach of trust.

For all these sins, forgiving God, forgive us, pardon us, grant us atonement.

We shall see in a moment that some of the rabbis of the Talmud refer to parts of what now serves as our Confession of sins for the Day of Atonement. Part of their work is to select among different versions of prayers already available the ones they think should be said in the synagogue. Another task is to make up prayers for people to say. Since the rabbis of the Talmud are both learned and holy, they have special gifts for creating prayers. Still, Jews at all later periods in the history of the Jewish people have joined in this never-ending work.

The first of the two units of the Talmud deals with the time at which we are supposed to say the confession.

A. Our rabbis have taught:

B. The religious duty [to say] the confession [applies] on the eve of the Day of Atonement, at dusk.

C. But said sages:

D. Let one say the confession before he eats and drinks,

E. lest one be upset during the meal.

F. And even though he said the confession before he ate and drank,

G. he should say the confession after he eats and drinks,

H. lest some mishap took place during the meal.

I. And even though he said the confession in the evening service,

J. let him say the confession in the morning service;

K. in the morning service, let him say the confession in the additional service;

L. in the additional service, let him say the confession in the afternoon service;

M. in the afternoon service, let him say it in the closing service.

N. And where [in the service] does he say it?

ת"ר

מִצְוַת

וִדּוּי עֶרֶב

יוה"כ עִם חֲשֵׁכָה.

אֲבָל אָמְרוּ חֲכָמִים:

יִתְוַדֶּה

קוֹדֶם שֶׁיֹּאכַל וְיִשְׁתֶּה,

שֶׁמָּא תִּטָּרֵף דַּעְתּוֹ

בִּסְעוּדָה.

ואע"פ שֶׁהִתְוַדָּה

קוֹדֶם שֶׁאָכַל

וְשָׁתָה,

מִתְוַדֶּה לְאַחַר

שֶׁיֹּאכַל וְיִשְׁתֶּה,

שֶׁמָּא אֵירַע דְּבָר קַלְקָלָה.

בִּסְעוּדָה.

וְאַף עַל פִּי

שֶׁהִתְוַדָּה עַרְבִית,

יִתְוַדֶּה

שַׁחֲרִית,

שַׁחֲרִית,

יִתְוַדֶּה

בְּמוּסָף,

בְּמוּסָף,

יִתְוַדֶּה

בְּמִנְחָה,

בְּמִנְחָה,

יִתְוַדֶּה בִּנְעִילָה.

וְהֵיכָן

אוֹמְרוֹ

O. An individual [praying by himself or herself] [says it] after the [silent] Prayer.

יָחִיד אַחַר תְּפִלָּתוֹ

P. And the agent of the congregation says it in the middle [of the Prayer].

וְשָׁלִיחַ צִבּוּר אוֹמְרוֹ בָּאֶמְצַע.

Vocabulary

religious duty	מִצְוָה
confession	וִידּוּי
the Day of Atonement	יוה״כ (יוֹם הַכִּפּוּרִים)
dusk	חֲשֵׁכָה
become upset	תִּטָּרֵף דַּעֲתוֹ
meal	סְעוּדָה
even though	אע״פ (אַף עַל פִּי)
he says confession	מִתְוַדֶּה
after	לְאַחַר
took place	אִירַע
mishap	דְּבַר קַלְקָלָה
evening service	עַרְבִית
morning service	שַׁחֲרִית
additional service	מוּסָף
afternoon service	מִנְחָה
closing service	נְעִילָה
individual	יָחִיד
his Prayer	תְּפִלָּתוֹ
agent of the congregation	שָׁלִיחַ צִבּוּר
in the middle	בָּאֶמְצַע

he *baraita,* stated in simple, tight clauses, has its own rhythm. Can you see it? Read the passage out loud, and you should be able to hear it. The *baraita* is arranged in matching clauses, which you can pick out (I-J, K-L, etc.). In fact, the *baraita* is divided into three parts. You can tell one from the other in two ways.

First, the subjects of the two are different.

Second, the two parts are phrased differently.

These go together, hand in hand: what is said and the way it is said. The three parts are A-H, I-M, and N-P. The first two parts are so neatly stated that we pass from the one to the other without any real break. Then the third part is set off by a question (N). But the whole is a single, coherent statement: When do we say the Confession? How often do we say the Confession? At what point in the service do we say the Confession?

The main point (A-H) is that one should say the confession prior to eating the final meal before sunset on the eve of the Day of Atonement. That way you may be sure that you have said the Confession correctly. You might have too much to drink at supper. Then, at the Kol Nidre service, you might miss something or make a mistake. That good advice leaves the impression that we say the Confession only once. So I-M hastens to tell us that we say it at each and every service for the Day of Atonement: Evening (which we call, *Kol Nidre*), Morning (*Shaharit*), Additional (*Musaf*), After-noon (*Minhah*), and Closing Service (*Neilah*)—five times in all.

The final question is where in the service one says the Confession. We recall that the service is said both by an individual and by a leader of the congregation in behalf of the whole community. So the silent prayer is said twice, once by ourselves, the second time by the agent of the congregation. When we say it by ourselves (O), we say it at the end of the silent Prayer. The agent of the congregation says it in the middle of the Prayer.

And precisely what is this Confession? Now we shall see something quite surprising. The rabbis of the Talmud have a number of different versions of the Confession. That means that in Talmudic times (and for a very long time afterward), people said many different kinds of prayers. Nothing was uniform. Moreover, it seems that the great rabbis—and other people as well—felt entirely free to contribute to the existing service. At the same time, of course, the discussion we just reviewed tells us that the service already had achieved a basic and unchangeable form, a normal structure, that might then be ornamented and embellished. But the basic order of prayer including the *Shema'* and the silent Prayer was fixed.

Q. What does one say?	מַאי אָמַר?
R. Said Rab, "You know the secrets of eternity. . . ."	אָמַר רַב, אַתָּה יוֹדֵעַ רָזֵי עוֹלָם...
S. And Samuel said, "From the depths of the heart. . . ."	וּשְׁמוּאֵל אָמַר, מִמַּעֲמַקֵּי הַלֵּב...
T. And Levi said, "In your Torah, it is said. . . ."	וְלֵוִי אָמַר, וּבְתוֹרָתְךָ כָּתוּב לֵאמֹר...
U. R. Yohanan said, "The Lord of all worlds. . . ."	ר׳ יוֹחָנָן אָמַר, רִבּוֹן הָעוֹלָמִים...
V. R. Judah said, Our iniquities are too many to count, and our sins too numerous to be counted.	ר׳ יְהוּדָה אָמַר, כִּי עֲוֹנוֹתֵינוּ רָבוּ מִלִּמְנוֹת וְחַטֹּאתֵינוּ עָצְמוּ מִסַפֵּר.
W. Rab Hamnuna said, "My God, before I was formed, I was of no worth. And now that I have been formed, it is as if I have not been formed. I am dust in my own life, how much more in my death. Behold, I am before you, like a dish full of shame and reproach. May it be your will that I sin no more, and what I have sinned, wipe away in your mercy, but not through suffering.	רַב הַמְנוּנָא אָמַר, אֱלֹהַי עַד שֶׁלֹּא נוֹצַרְתִּי אֵינִי כְדָאי, עַכְשָׁיו שֶׁנּוֹצַרְתִּי כְּאִילוּ לֹא נוֹצַרְתִּי. עָפָר אֲנִי בְּחַיַּי ק״ו (קַל וָחֹמֶר) בְּמִיתָתִי. הֲרֵי אֲנִי לְפָנֶיךָ כִּכְלִי מָלֵא בּוּשָׁה וּכְלִימָה. יְהִי רָצוֹן מִלְּפָנֶיךָ שֶׁלֹּא אֶחֱטָא, וּמַה שֶׁחָטָאתִי, מְחֹק בְּרַחֲמֶיךָ, אֲבָל לֹא עַ״י (עַל יְדֵי) יִסּוּרִין.

X. And this is the confession of Rabah during the entire year,	וְהַיְינוּ וִידוּיָא דְּרָבָא כּוּלָהּ שַׁתָּא
Y. and of Rab Hamnuna the Lesser on the Day of Atonement.	וּדְרַב הַמְנוּנָא זוּטָא בְּיוֹמָא דְּכִפּוּרֵי.

Vocabulary

what	מַאי
know	יוֹדֵעַ
the secrets of the world	רָזֵי עוֹלָם
from the depths of the heart	מִמַּעֲמַקֵּי הַלֵּב
your Torah	תּוֹרָתְךָ
Lord of all worlds	רִבּוֹן הָעוֹלָמִים
our iniquities	עֲונוֹתֵינוּ
to count	לִמְנוֹת
our sins	חֲטָאתֵינוּ
too numerous	עָצְמוּ
to be counted	מִסְפָּר
before I was formed	עַד שֶׁלֹּא נוֹצַרְתִּי
I was of no worth	אֵינִי כְדַאי
now	עַכְשָׁיו
I have been formed	נוֹצַרְתִּי
it is as if	כְּאִילוּ
dust	עָפָר
how much the more so	ק״ו (קַל וָחוֹמֶר)
my death	מִיתָתִי
dish	כְּלִי
full	מָלֵא
shame	בּוּשָׁה
reproach	כְּלִימָה
I will sin	אֶחֱטָא

wipe away	מְחק
your mercy	רַחֲמֶיךָ
through	עַ״י (עַל יְדֵי)
suffering	יִסּוּרִין
the entire year	כּוּלָה שַׁתָּא

ow many proposals do we have for the text of the Confession? I count five: Rab (R), Samuel (S), Levi (T), Yohanan (U), Judah (V), and Hamnuna (W). Then at the end we have an expected conclusion. We are told what some people actually said as the confession (X and Y).

What are the prayers of Confession alluded to by the five rabbis before us?

Rab refers us to the prayer, "You know the mysteries of the universe." This is the one translated by Rabbi Harlow. Samuel's appears to be the same prayer, except that Samuel knows the introductory words as, "You know the depths of the heart." Levi's prayer appears to correspond to the prayer we say in the silent Prayer of the Day of Atonement, in Rabbi Harlow's translation:

Our God and God of our fathers, forgive our sins on this Day of Atonement. Blot out and disregard our transgressions, as Isaiah declared in Your name, "I alone blot out your transgressions, for My sake your sins I shall not recall. I have swept away your transgressions like a cloud, your sins like mist. Return to Me, for I have redeemed you. And the Torah promises, For on this day atonement shall be made for you, to cleanse you; of all your sins before the Lord shall you be cleansed.

We may readily see why this prayer would be relevant to the Mishnah with which we began so long ago. As you notice, precisely the same biblical verse is important to both the Mishnah and the prayer of Confession as Levi cites it.

This brings us to Yohanan's prayer of Confession. It occurs, in fact, in

149

every Morning Service of the year, again in Rabbi Harlow's translation:

> Lord of all worlds! Not upon our merit do we rely in supplication, but upon
> Your boundless compassion. What are we? What is our piety? What is our
> righteousness? What is our attainment, our power, our might? What can we
> say, Lord our God and God of our fathers? Compared to You, all the mighty
> are nothing, the famous are non-existent, the wise lack wisdom, the clever
> lack reason. For most of their actions are meaninglessness, the days of their
> lives emptiness. Man's superiority to the beast is an illusion. All life is a
> fleeting breath.

If you look back at the Confession now in our *Mahzor*, you will see that
Yohanan's opinion is certainly taken into account. For the Confession to
which he refers is included in the paragraph beginning, *You know our sins.*
Judah's sentence would not seem to occur in our Confession. Hamnuna
spells out the prayer as he wants it to be said. This prayer now occurs at the
end of the silent Prayer of the Day of Atonement, at the conclusion of the
Confession.

It appears that the several proposals before us in the Talmud have made
their way into the *Mahzor* as we know it.

If we now look back at our Mishnah-passage, we see that the Talmud
has essentially gone its own way. We have seen this before. While the Mishnah provides the point of departure, it does not indicate the only road to be
followed. As we know, the rabbis of the Talmud do not hesitate to explore
issues, ideas or problems important to them but which are not raised in the
Mishnah-passage on which they are working. This is another sign of the
essential independence and freedom of the rabbis who created the Talmud.
They are deeply loyal to the Mishnah. They are eager to clarify it. They
want to be sure that every one of its words is defined. They make certain that
any questions left open in the Mishnah-passage under discussion will be
answered thoroughly and that the answers themselves will be fully explained.

But they do go their own way. They ask their own questions. Obviously, at this point in their treatment of our Mishnah-passage, they have not
strayed far from the basic theme, which is the Day of Atonement and the
forgiveness of sins. But we see that they also introduce the subjects important in their own day, not only in the time in which the Mishnah was made
up. That is why they can ask about what Confession we say on the Day of
Atonement, when we say it, and which of the available versions we are

supposed to say.

Yet if you look at the *Mahzor* as we know it, you will see that other people have been just as independent of the Talmudic rabbis as those rabbis were from the authorities of the Mishnah. For we have a Confession that incorporates the ideas of some of the rabbis before us but that also goes its own way.

And that is the way of the Torah laid out by the rabbis of the Talmud. They read the written Torah and claim to provide yet another Torah—the Mishnah, the Oral Torah. But then later rabbis come along and treat the oral Torah as a completion of the written Torah, not as an independent part of the Torah, which, for its part, it would seem to want to be. For what the Mishnah says on its own authority, the Talmud demands scriptural foundations, a verse in the written Torah.

The Talmud, too, would undergo in time the same experience. It would be received with care and reverence, but it would not prevent those who received it from responding, in their own fresh and interesting ways, to what it said.

That is why at the outset we spoke not of asking for answers but of using our own minds to discover the answers. The experience of learning the Talmud teaches the lesson that we must always stand back and make up our own minds. We must always discover for ourselves those things that in the end, we shall affirm and believe. We do not merely ask other people to tell us what is so. We must find out for ourselves. And the only way in which we can find out for ourselves is by using our own minds and not by relying upon other people—however learned or holy, however much we admire and wish to follow them—to give us answers.

22. The Talmud All Together

BABYLONIAN TALMUD YOMA 87A-B (EXCERPT)

For the last time we look at the entire passage, Mishnah and Talmud, and ask how it has been put together. Since we deal with two distinct excerpts, we cannot answer that question as it applies to the entire passage. We deal with the two large units we have examined. First, how does the Talmud treat the Mishnah-passage with which we started? Second, how does the Talmud then expand on the topic of the Mishnah-passage? We now know that the Talmud does two things.

First, it most certainly *does* explain the Mishnah-passage, but in its own way. It answers questions the Mishnah-passage raises, but it does so in a fresh and subtle manner.

Second, the Talmud will not stop within the boundaries of the Mishnah-passage. The editor of the pages of the Talmud under study here does not hesitate to use materials relevant to the Mishnah in only a general way.

Do you see any real relationship between the two operations: explanation of the Mishnah, expansion of the explanation? Is the process of making peace with our friend, whom we have hurt, related to the confession that we say in our prayers? When we ask that question, we once more ask a basic question about the Talmud, as well as a basic question about the contents of the Talmud. Is the Talmud more than an anthology? Is the lesson of the Talmud more than a sequence of unrelated thoughts?

The answer is not difficult to see. In fact, once you have reread the two distinct passages, you should find the answer self-evident.

1	He who says	הָאוֹמֵר:
	I shall sin and repent, sin and repent	אֶחֱטָא וְאָשׁוּב, אֶחֱטָא וְאָשׁוּב -
	they do not give him sufficient power to make repentance	אֵין מַסְפִּיקִין בְּיָדוֹ לַעֲשׂוֹת תְּשׁוּבָה;
	[He who says], I shall sin, and	אֶחֱטָא, וְיוֹם הַכִּפּוּרִים מְכַפֵּר -

152

the Day of Atonement will
atone

the Day of Atonement does not
atone.

אֵין יוֹם הַכִּפּוּרִים מְכַפֵּר.

2   Sins which are between man
and the Omnipresent

the Day of Atonement atones
for.

Sins which are between man
and his fellow

the Day of Atonement does not
atone for

until one will win the good
will of his fellow [once
more].

עֲבֵרוֹת שֶׁבֵּין אָדָם לַמָּקוֹם -

יוֹם הַכִּפּוּרִים מְכַפֵּר;

עֲבֵרוֹת שֶׁבֵּין אָדָם לַחֲבֵרוֹ -

אֵין יוֹם הַכִּפּוּרִים מְכַפֵּר,

עַד שֶׁיְרַצֶּה אֶת חֲבֵרוֹ.

3   This is what Rabbi Eleazar ben
Azariah expounded:

From all your sins shall you be
clean before the Lord (Lev.
16:3)

Sins which are between man
and the Omnipresent

the Day of Atonement atones
for.

Sins which are between man
and his fellow

the Day of Atonement does not
atone for

until one will win the good
will of his fellow.

אֶת זוֹ דָּרַשׁ רַבִּי אֶלְעָזָר בֶּן עֲזַרְיָה:

„מִכֹּל חַטֹּאתֵיכֶם לִפְנֵי ה׳ תִּטְהָרוּ";

עֲבֵרוֹת שֶׁבֵּין אָדָם לַמָּקוֹם -

יוֹם הַכִּפּוּרִים מְכַפֵּר.

עֲבֵרוֹת שֶׁבֵּין אָדָם לַחֲבֵרוֹ -

אֵין יוֹם הַכִּפּוּרִים מְכַפֵּר,

עַד שֶׁיְרַצֶּה אֶת חֲבֵרוֹ.

4   Said Rabbi 'Aqiva
Happy are you, Oh Israel!

אָמַר רַבִּי עֲקִיבָא:
אַשְׁרֵיכֶם יִשְׂרָאֵל!

Before whom are you purified?	לִפְנֵי מִי אַתֶּם מְטַהֲרִין?
Who purifies you?	מִי מְטַהֵר אֶתְכֶם?
Your father who is in heaven.	אֲבִיכֶם שֶׁבַּשָּׁמַיִם,
As it is said, And I will sprinkle clean water on you and you will be clean (Ezekiel 36:25).	שֶׁנֶּאֱמַר: „וְזָרַקְתִּי עֲלֵיכֶם מַיִם טְהוֹרִים וּטְהַרְתֶּם";
And it says, "The hope of Israel is the Lord (Jeremiah 17:13)."	וְאוֹמֵר: „מִקְוֵה יִשְׂרָאֵל ה'";
Just as the immersion-pool cleans the unclean people,	מַה הַמִּקְוֶה מְטַהֵר אֶת הַטְּמֵאִים,
So the Holy One blessed be he cleans Israel.	אַף הַקָּדוֹשׁ בָּרוּךְ הוּא מְטַהֵר אֶת יִשְׂרָאֵל.
I. A. Said R. Isaac,	אָמַר ר' יִצְחָק,
B. Whoever offends his fellow,	כָּל הַמַּקְנִיט אֶת חֲבֵירוֹ,
C. even [merely] through words,	אֲפִילוּ בִּדְבָרִים,
D. has to make peace with him,	צָרִיךְ לְפַיְּסוֹ,
E. since it is said,	שֶׁנֶּאֱמַר,
F. My son, if you have become a surety for your neighbor, if you have struck your hands for a stranger, you are snared by the words of your mouth. Do this now, my son, and deliver yourself, since you have come into the hand of your neighbor. Go, humble yourself, and urge your neighbor (Prov. 6:1-3).	בְּנִי אִם עָרַבְתָּ לְרֵעֶךָ, תָּקַעְתָּ לַזָּר כַּפֶּיךָ, נוֹקַשְׁתָּ בְאִמְרֵי פִיךָ. עֲשֵׂה זֹאת אֵפוֹא בְנִי וְהִנָּצֵל, כִּי בָאתָ בְכַף רֵעֶךָ. לֵךְ הִתְרַפֵּס וּרְהַב רֵעֶיךָ.
G. If you are wealthy	אִם מָמוֹן יֵשׁ בְּיָדְךָ

154

H. open the palm of your hand to him.	הַתֵּר לוֹ פִּסַת יָד,
I. And if not	וְאִם לָאו,
J. send many friends to him.	הַרְכֵּב עָלָיו רֵעִים.
K. Said R. Hisda,	אָמַר רַב חִסְדָּא,
L. And he needs to make peace with him through three groups of three people,	וְצָרִיךְ לְפַיְּיסוֹ בְּשָׁלֹשׁ שׁוּרוֹת שֶׁל שְׁלֹשָׁה בְנֵי אָדָם,
M. since it is said,	שֶׁנֶּאֱמַר,
N. He comes before men and says,	יָשׁוֹר עַל אֲנָשִׁים וַיֹּאמֶר
O. I have sinned, and I have perverted that which was right, and it did me no profit (Job 33:27).	חָטָאתִי, וְיָשָׁר הֶעֱוֵיתִי, וְלֹא שָׁוָה לִי.
P. Said R. Yose b. R. Hanina,	(וְאָמַר) ר׳ יוֹסֵי בַּר חֲנִינָא,
Q. Whoever seeks pardon of his fellow	כָּל הַמְבַקֵּשׁ מָטוּ מֵחֲבֵירוֹ.
R. should not seek it from him more than three times,	אַל יְבַקֵּשׁ מִמֶּנּוּ יוֹתֵר מִשָּׁלֹשׁ פְּעָמִים,
S. since it is said, Forgive, I pray you now, and now we pray you (Gen. 50:17).	שֶׁנֶּאֱמַר, אָנָּא שָׂא נָא ... וְעַתָּה שָׂא נָא.
T. But if he dies,	וְאִם מֵת,
U. one brings ten men,	מֵבִיא עֲשָׂרָה בְּנֵי אָדָם
V. and sets them up at his grave,	וּמַעֲמִידָן עַל קִבְרוֹ,
W. and says,	וְאוֹמֵר,
Y. "I have sinned against the Lord, the God of Israel,	חָטָאתִי לַה׳ אֱלֹהֵי יִשְׂרָאֵל
Z. "and against Mr. So and So, whom I have injured."	וְלִפְלוֹנִי שֶׁחָבַלְתִּי בוֹ.

II.   A. R. Jeremiah had something against R. Abba.

ר׳ יִרְמְיָה הֲוָה לֵיה מִילְתָא לר׳ אַבָּא בַּהֲדֵיה

B. He went and sat down at the door of R. Abba.

אָזַל אֵיתִיב אַדַּשָׁא דר׳ אַבָּא.

C. As the maid was throwing out water,

בַּהֲדֵי דְשָׁדְיָא אַמְתֵיה מַיָּא,

D. a few drops of water touched his head.

מְטָא זַרְזִיפֵי דְמַיָּא אַרֵישָׁא.

E. He said, They have made me into a dung-heap.

אֲמַר עֲשָׂאוּנִי כְּאַשְׁפָּה.

F. He cited the following verse about himself:

קְרָא אַנַּפְשֵׁיה:

G. He raises up the poor out of the dust (I Samuel 2:8).

מֵאַשְׁפּוֹת יָרִים אֶבְיוֹן.

H. R. Abba heard.

שָׁמַע ר׳ אַבָּא

I. And he came to him.

וּנְפִיק לְאַפֵּיה.

J. He said to him,

אֲמַר לֵיה,

K. Now I must make peace with you.

הַשְׁתָּא צְרִיכְנָא לְמֵיפַק אַדַּעְתָּךְ

L. For it is written,

דִּכְתִיב,

M. Go, humble yourself and urge your neighbor (Prov. 6:3).

לֵךְ הִתְרַפֵּס וּרְהַב רֵעֶיךָ.

III. A. R. Zeira, when he had something against some one,

ר׳ זֵירָא כִּי הֲוָה לֵיה מִילְתָא בַּהֲדֵי אִינִישׁ

B. would go back and forth before him,

הֲוָה חָלֵיף וְתָנֵי לְקַמֵיה

C. and make himself available to the other,

וּמַמְצִיא לֵיה,

D. so that the other would come out

כִּי הֵיכִי דְנֵיתִי

E. and make peace with him.

וְנִיפּוֹק לֵיה מִדַּעְתֵּיה.

IV. A. Rab [= Rab Abba] had something against a certain butcher.

רַב הֲוָה לֵיהּ

B. He [the butcher] did not come to him [Rab].

מִילְתָא בַּהֲדֵי הַהוּא טַבָּחָא; לָא אָתָא לְקַמֵיהּ.

C. On the eve of the Day of Atonement, he [Rab] said, I shall go to make peace with him.

בְּמַעֲלֵי יוֹמָא דְכִפּוּרֵי אָמַר אִיהוּ אֵיזִיל אֲנָא לְפַיּוֹסֵי לֵיהּ.

D. R. Huna met him.

פָּגַע בֵּיהּ רַב הוּנָא.

E. He said to him, Where is the master going?

אָמַר לֵיהּ לְהֵיכָא קָא אָזֵיל מָר,

F. He said to him, "To make peace with so-and-so."

אָמַר לֵיהּ לְפַיּוֹסֵי לִפְלַנְיָא.

G. He said, "Abba is going to kill someone."

אָמַר אָזֵיל אַבָּא לְמִיקְטַל נַפְשָׁא.

H. He [Rab] went and stood before him.

אָזַל וְקָם עִילָוֵיהּ.

I. He [the butcher] was sitting and chopping an [animal's] head.

הֲוָה יָתֵיב וְקָא סָלֵי רֵישָׁא.

J. He [the butcher] raised his eyes and saw him.

דַּלֵי עֵינֵיהּ וְחַזְיֵיהּ,

K. He said to him, "You are Abba! Get out. I have nothing to do with you."

אָמַר לֵיהּ אַבָּא אַתְּ זִיל, לֵית לִי מִילְתָא בַּהֲדָךְ.

L. While he was chopping the head,

בַּהֲדֵי דְּקָא סָלֵי רֵישָׁא

M. a bone flew off,

אִישְׁתַּמֵּיט גַּרְמָא

N. and stuck his throat,

וּמְחַיֵיהּ בְּקוֹעֵיהּ,

O. and killed him.

וְקַטְלֵיהּ.

V. A. Our rabbis have taught:

ת"ר

B. The religious duty [to say] the confession [applies] on

מִצְוַת וִידּוּי עֶרֶב

157

the eve of the Day of
Atonement, at dusk.

C. But said sages:

D. Let one say the confession
before he eats and drinks,

E. lest one be upset during the
meal.

F. And even though he said
the confession before he ate
and drank,

G. he should say the
confession after he eats and
drinks,

H. lest some mishap took
place during the meal.

I. And even though he said
the confession in the
evening service,

J. let him say the confession in
the morning service:

K. in the morning service, let
him say the confession in the
additional service;

L. in the additional service,
let him say the confession in
the afternoon service;

M. in the afternoon service,
let him say it in the closing
service.

N. And where [in the service]
does he say it?

O. An individual [praying by
himself or herself] [says it]
after the [silent] Prayer.

P. And the agent of the

יוה״כ עִם חֲשֵׁכָה.

אֲבָל אָמְרוּ חֲכָמִים:

יִתְוַדֶּה
קוֹדֶם שֶׁיֹּאכַל וְיִשְׁתֶּה,

שֶׁמָּא תִּטָּרֵף דַּעְתּוֹ
בַּסְּעוּדָה.

ואע״פ שֶׁהִתְוַדָה
קוֹדֶם שֶׁאָכַל
וְשָׁתָה,

מִתְוַדֶּה לְאַחַר
שֶׁיֹּאכַל וְיִשְׁתֶּה,

שֶׁמָּא אֵירַע דְּבַר קַלְקָלָה.
בַּסְּעוּדָה.

וְאַף עַל פִּי
שֶׁהִתְוַדָה עַרְבִית,

יִתְוַדֶּה
שַׁחֲרִית,

שַׁחֲרִית,
יִתְוַדֶּה
בְּמוּסָף,

בְּמוּסָף,
יִתְוַדֶּה
בְּמִנְחָה,

בְּמִנְחָה,
יִתְוַדֶּה בִּנְעִילָה.

וְהֵיכָן
אוֹמְרוֹ
יָחִיד
אַחַר
תְּפִלָּתוֹ
וּשְׁלִיחַ

158

congregation says it in the middle [of the Prayer].

Q. What does one say?

R. Said Rab, "You know the secrets of eternity . . ."

S. And Samuel said, "From the depths of the heart . . ."

T. And Levi said, "In your Torah, it is said . . ."

U. R. Yohanan said, "Lord of all worlds . . ."

V. R. Judah said, Our iniquities are too many to count, and our sins too numerous to be counted.

W. Rab Hamnuna said, "My God, before I was formed, I was of no worth. And now that I have been formed, it is as if I have not been formed. I am dust in my own life, how much more in my death. Behold, I am before you, like a dish full of shame and reproach. May it be your will that I sin no more, and what I have sinned, wipe away in your mercy, but not through suffering.

X. And this is the confession of Rabbah during the entire year,

Y. and of Rab Hamnuna the Lesser on the Day of Atonement.

צִבּוּר אוֹמְרוֹ בָּאֶמְצַע.

מַאי אָמַר?

אָמַר רַב, אַתָּה יוֹדֵעַ רָזֵי עוֹלָם...

וּשְׁמוּאֵל אָמַר, מִמַּעֲמַקֵּי הַלֵּב...

וְלֵוִי אָמַר, וּבְתוֹרָתְךָ כָּתוּב לֵאמֹר...

ר׳ יוֹחָנָן אָמַר, רִבּוֹן הָעוֹלָמִים...

ר׳ יְהוּדָה אָמַר, כִּי עֲוֹנוֹתֵינוּ רָבוּ מִלִּמְנוֹת וְחַטֹּאתֵינוּ עָצְמוּ מִסַּפֵּר.

רַב הַמְנוּנָא אָמַר, אֱלֹהַי עַד שֶׁלֹּא נוֹצַרְתִּי אֵינִי כְדַאי, עַכְשָׁיו שֶׁנּוֹצַרְתִּי כְּאִילּוּ לֹא נוֹצַרְתִּי. עָפָר אֲנִי בְּחַיַּי ק״ו (קַל וָחוֹמֶר) בְּמִיתָתִי. הֲרֵי אֲנִי לְפָנֶיךָ כִּכְלִי מָלֵא בּוּשָׁה וּכְלִימָה. יְהִי רָצוֹן מִלְּפָנֶיךָ שֶׁלֹּא אֶחֱטָא, וּמַה שֶּׁחָטָאתִי, מְחֹק בְּרַחֲמֶיךָ, אֲבָל לֹא עַ״י (עַל יְדֵי) יִסּוּרִין.

וְהַיְינוּ וִידּוּיָא דְרַבָּא כּוּלָהּ שַׁתָּא

וּדְרַב הַמְנוּנָא זוּטָא בְּיוֹמָא דְכִפּוּרֵי.

e expand the Mishnah-passage by explaining how we appease someone we have harmed. The story concludes with Rab's actions on the eve of the Day of Atonement. The Mishnah-passage would be happy at this point. Then, we proceed and confess our sins. This, of course, is much more relevant to the Day of Atonement. We refer directly and explicitly to the prayers we say in the synagogue on that awesome day. So what has the Talmud told us?

First, prepare for worship on the Day of Atonement. This you do by your behavior toward your friends.

Second, worship on the Day of Atonement, say prayers that refer to our behavior both to our friends and to God.

It would be difficult to imagine a more complete account of our theme. First, prepare yourself to do. Second, while doing, refer back to your preparation. Correct your sins as much as possible, then confess your sins so God can do the rest.

The basic idea would not have surprised the rabbis who told us what blessings we say when we enjoy benefits of the world, and how God blesses us for doing God's will—studying Torah. The main point is before us, spread out on a different field, but familiar. It is that the will of God is to love God's creation and respect God's creatures, who are our fellow human beings. God's will is revealed to us in the Torah, which, therefore, we must study.

The Confessions of the several rabbis should strike you in one more way; they stress the humility that characterizes the rabbis who are the greatest masters of Torah. These are not proud but humble men. Their Torah study and their practice of the teachings of Torah—the commandments—result not in a sense of knowing and doing just what they should know and do. There is not much talk about how grand we are. Rabbis do not congratulate themselves for what they know and do. They underline their own failures; they are aware of their sins and transgressions. Rabbis humbly seek forgiveness of ordinary folk who have been hurt by them.

160

When the butcher acts in a mean way, it is Heaven who punishes him.

These are some of the things that a reading of the entire passage calls to our minds. Let us now, for the last time, read the passage as it appears in the Talmud. You should be able to supply the needed periods and commas and be able to recognize the points at which one unit of thought—one paragraph—comes to an end and another begins.

האומר: אחטא ואשוב, אחטא ואשוב - אין מספיקין בידו לעשות תשובה; אחטא, ויום הכפורים מכפר - אין יום הכפורים מכפר. עברות שבין אדם למקום - יום הכפורים מכפר; עברות שבין אדם לחברו - אין יום הכפורים מכפר, עד שירצה את חברו. את זו דרש רבי אלעזר בן עזריה: ״מכל חטאתיכם לפני-ה׳ תטהרו״; עברות שבין אדם למקום - יום הכפורים מכפר; עברות שבין אדם לחברו - אין יום הכפורים מכפר, עד שירצה את חברו. אמר רבי עקיבא: אשריכם ישראל! לפני מי אתם מטהרין? מי מטהר אתכם? אביכם שבשמים, שנאמר: ״וזרקתי עליכם מים טהורים וטהרתם״; ואומר: ״מקוה ישראל ה׳״; מה המקוה מטהר את הטמאים, אף הקדוש ברוך הוא מטהר את ישראל.

אמר ר׳ יצחק כל המקניט את חבירו אפילו בדברים צריך לפייסו שנאמר בני אם ערבת לרעך תקעת לזר כפיך נוקשת באמרי פיך עשה זאת אפוא בני והנצל כי באת בכף רעך לך התרפס ורהב רעיך אם ממון יש בידך התר לו פסת יד ואם לאו הברה עליו ריעים (ואמר) רב חסדא וצריך לפייסו בשלש שורות של שלשה בני אדם שנאמר ישור על אנשים ויאמר חטאתי וישר העויתי ולא שוה לי (ואמר) ר׳ יוסי בר חנינא כל המבקש מטו מחבירו אל יבקש ממנו יותר משלש פעמים שנאמר אנא שא נא ועתה שא נא ואם מת מביא עשרה בני אדם ומעמידן על קברו ואומר חטאתי לה׳ אלהי ישראל ולפלוני שחבלתי בו ר׳ ירמיה הוה ליה מילתא לר׳ אבא בהדיה אזל איתיב אדשא דר׳ אבא בהדי דשדיא אמתיה מיא מטא

161

זרזיפי דמיא ארישא אמר עשאוני כאשפה קרא אנפשיה
מאשפות ירים אביין שמע ר' אבא ונפיק לאפיה אמר ליה השתא
צריכנא למיפק אדעתך דכתיב לך התרפס ורהב רעיך ר' זירא כי
הוה ליה מילתא בהדי איניש הוה חליף ותני לקמיה וממציא ליה
כי היכי דניתי וניפוק ליה מרדעתיה רב הוה ליה מילתא בהדי ההוא
טבחא לא אתא לקמיה במעלי יומא דכפורי אמר איהו איזיל אנא
לפיוסי ליה פגע ביה רב הונא אמר ליה להיכא קא אזיל מר אמר
ליה לפיוסי לפלניא אמר אזיל אבא למיקטל נפשא אזל וקם
עילויה הוה יתיב וקא פלי רישא דלי עיניה וחזייה אמר ליה אבא
את זיל לית לי מילתא בהדך דקא פלי רישא אישתמיט גרמא
ומחייה בקועיה וקטליה

ת"ר מצות וידוי ערב יוה"כ עם חשכה אבל אמרו חכמים יתודה
קודם שיאכל וישתה שמא תטרף דעתו בסעודה ואע"פ שהתודה
קודם שאכל ושתה מתודה לאחר שיאכל וישתה שמא שמא אירע דבר
קלקלה בסעודה ואף על פי שהתודה ערבית יתודה שחרית
שחרית יתודה במוסף במוסף יתודה במנחה במנחה יתודה
בנעילה והיכן אומרין יחיד אחר תפלתו ושליח צבור אומרו באמצע
מאי אמר רב אתה יודע רזי עולם ושמואל אמר ממעמקי הלב
ולוי אמר ובתורתך כתוב לאמר ר' יוחנן אמר רבון העולמים ר'
יהודה אמר כי עונותינו רבו מלמנות וחטאתינו עצמו מספר רב
המנונא אמר אלהי עד שלא נוצרתי איני כדאי עכשיו שנוצרתי
כאילו לא נוצרתי עפר אני בחיי ק"ו במיתתי הרי אני לפניך ככלי
מלא בושה וכלימה יהי רצון מלפניך שלא אחטא ומה שחטאתי
מחק ברחמיך אבל לא ע"י יסורין והיינו וידויא דרבא כולה שתא
ודרב המנונא זוטא ביומא דכפורי

e now ask for the fourth and last time, "Has the Talmud said important things about the Mishnah? Or has the Talmud said essentially trivial and unimportant things?"

The Talmud has done two things. First, it has said important things about the Mishnah. Second, it has made the Mishnah still more important than it was. The Talmud has not left up in the air the matter of seeking forgiveness on the Day of Atonement. The Talmud has brought things down to earth by providing us with prayers we ourselves may, and do, say. So the Talmud makes concrete and everyday what, in the present instance, the Mishnah-passage has left somewhere between heaven and earth.

We conclude with the point at which we started—the relationship, in the Mishnah and the Talmud, between believing and behaving, between *aggadah* and *halakhah*. The Mishnah speaks about the meaning of the Day of Atonement and what it can and cannot do for us. The Talmud spells out that meaning in terms of everyday actions. But the Talmud does not leave things in the world of rules and laws, of *halakhah*. That is what it adds to the *aggadah* of the Mishnah. When the Talmud gives us rules, it also gives us *aggadah* of its own—a repertoire of prayers that we may say.

These prayers are deep and penetrate to the foundations of our inner life. Are they *halakhah* or *aggadah*? They are both. They are words we are supposed to say. The prayers, as prayers, are a part of *halakhah*. But the prayers, as expressions of beliefs, are an account of what is in our hearts. They evoke a certain response from us, and by saying them, we hope to call a certain response from Heaven as well. We wisely conclude with what we said before. The deeds express our faith. The faith gives meaning to the deeds. There is no Mishnah without Talmud, no *halakhah* without *aggadah*, no *aggadah* without *halakhah*.

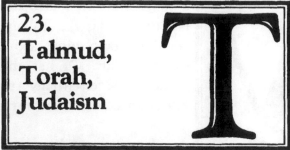

23.
Talmud, Torah, Judaism

MISHNAH ABOT 2:8 AND ABOT DERABBI NATHAN 14:2 (EXCERPT)

WHAT IS THE TALMUD?

The Talmud is an explanation and expansion of the Mishnah. The Talmud also is a carefully put together statement of its own. It says what it wants to say, in the name of the Mishnah and, so to speak, in its own name as well.

Why should someone want to know the Talmud? Why do a great many Jews today believe that the best time they have in this world is the time they spend "studying Torah," which means studying the Talmud? You remember how the ancient rabbis debated whether it is all right both to work for a living and to study Torah, or whether we should simply study Torah. Now you do not live in a world in which most Jews think that that is a pressing issue. Most Jews you are likely to know do not "study Torah," whatever they may mean by Torah.

True, they may spend a lot of time talking *about* "what it means to be a Jew." But they do not spend much time "being a Jew" as the rabbis of the Mishnah and the Talmud understand "being a Jew," which is "studying Torah." So it is fair to ask you to think about why anyone nowadays would want to study Torah in the sense of learning Mishnah and learning Talmud.

For if this book is going to succeed, it should make you want to continue the study of Torah that we have begun here. It will lead you to ask your teachers to teach you what you need to know, however long it takes, so that you, on your own, may study Torah in a responsible way.

Why?

It will not do to say, "because it is interesting because it tells me things I did not know but I want to know." There are easier ways to learn what we want to know than to learn Talmud. The real reason to do this work is not merely to gain information or even insight. For that purpose, you can rely on others.

I think the real reason is in two parts. Part of the right reason to study Torah is that it is a joy and fun! It is not the same sort of fun you have when you go swimming or play baseball. It is obviously a wholly other sort of thing. It engages your mind to get the results and to participate in this achievement. The job is in the work of discovery, not primarily in what is learned. The pleasure of studying Torah is in the act of studying. The reward of learning is the work of learning, and the work is its own reward.

The other part of the reason is that Judaism teaches that God wants us to study. I realize that that is a considerable statement, which one cannot prove. We only know that it is precisely what Yohanan ben Zakkai has told us in the Mishnah:

Rabban Yohanan ben Zakkai received [Torah] from Hillel and Shammai.	רַבָּן יוֹחָנָן בֶּן זַכַּאי קִבֵּל מֵהִלֵּל וּמִשַּׁמַאי.
He would say	הוּא הָיָה אוֹמֵר:
If you have learned much Torah	אִם לָמַדְתָּ תּוֹרָה הַרְבֵּה,
do not think well of yourself [on that account]	אַל תַּחֲזִיק טוֹבָה לְעַצְמָךְ,
for to that end were you created	כִּי לְכָךְ נוֹצָרְתָּ.

Vocabulary

received	קִבֵּל	for yourself	לְעַצְמָךְ
you learned	לָמַדְתָּ	because	כִּי
much	הַרְבֵּה	for this	לְכָךְ
do not	אַל	you were created	נוֹצָרְתָּ
claim	תַּחֲזִיק		

ohanan ben Zakkai's claim is all I can offer you: We are made to do this work.

This is what it means to be a human being in the community of Israel—the Jewish people. There is a kind of Talmud to Mishnah Abot,

165

and it is called, *The Fathers (Abot) according to Rabbi Nathan.* At the
end let us see how that Talmud adds to what Yohanan ben Zakkai says:

He would say:	הוּא הָיָה אוֹמֵר:
If you have studied much Torah,	אִם לָמַדְתָּ תּוֹרָה הַרְבֵּה,
do not think well of yourself [on that account]	אַל תַּחֲזִיק טוֹבָה לְעַצְמֶךָ,
For to that end were you created,	כִּי לְכָךְ נוֹצַרְתָּ.
because human beings were created only	לְפִי שֶׁלֹּא נוֹצְרוּ הַבְּרִיּוֹת אֶלָּא
on condition that they engage in Torah-study.	עַל מְנָת שֶׁיִּתְעַסְקוּ בַּתּוֹרָה

Vocabulary

because	לְפִי	only	לֹא...אֶלָּא
were created	נוֹצְרוּ	on condition	עַל מְנָת שֶׁ...
human beings	בְּרִיּוֹת	engage in	יִתְעַסְקוּ

We need not try to improve upon what Yohanan says, as the later master spells it out:

We are here on earth to study the Torah of Heaven. To put it simply: When we study Torah, we are doing what comes naturally. We are doing what we are made to do. Learning Mishnah and learning Talmud are holy deeds. We do them because we want to be holy, to be like God. That is our nature.